CLASSIC GUITARS

60s

CLASSIC GUITARS OF THE SIXTIES

MILLER FREEMAN BOOKS
FIRST AMERICAN EDITION 1997

PUBLISHED IN THE UK BY BALAFON BOOKS, AN IMPRINT OF OUTLINE PRESS LTD.
115J CLEVELAND STREET, LONDON W1P 5PN, ENGLAND.

PUBLISHED IN THE UNITED STATES BY MILLER FREEMAN BOOKS
600 HARRISON STREET, SAN FRANCISCO, CA 94107
PUBLISHERS OF 'GUITAR PLAYER' AND 'BASS PLAYER' MAGAZINES
MILLER FREEMAN, INC. IS A UNITED NEWS AND MEDIA COMPANY

un Miller Freeman
A United News & Media company

ISBN 0-87930-491-X

PRINTED IN HONG KONG

CREATIVE DIRECTOR: NIGEL OSBORNE
EDITOR: TONY BACON
DESIGN: SALLY STOCKWELL
PHOTOGRAPHY: MIKI SLINGSBY
PORTRAITS: ROB McCAIG

TYPESETTING BY KEVIN DODD & MICHAEL CUSHING AT TYPE TECHNIQUE, LONDON W1
PRINT & ORIGINATION BY REGENT PUBLISHING SERVICES

97 98 99 00 01 5 4 3 2 1

*This book is dedicated to the memory of my dad
and friend, Bill Bacon (1929-1996), who among many things
showed me how to love music – Tony Bacon.*

*"When loved ones die, you have to live on their behalf.
See things as through their eyes. Remember how they used to say
things, and use those words oneself. Be thankful that you can
do things that they cannot and also feel the sadness of it."
(Louis de Bernières, Captain Corelli's Mandolin.)*

CONTENTS

The guitars featured in this book are arranged chronologically and the story of the decade's musical developments, the players and their key recordings is told by leading international music writers in the following chapters:

INTRODUCTION *by Dave Gregory*   4

JAZZ GUITARS *by Charles Alexander*   11

AMERICAN GUITARS *by Tom Wheeler*   16

EUROPEAN GUITARS *by Paul Day*   22

RADIO & TELEVISION *by Michael Wright*   26

GIBSON GUITARS *by André Duchossoir*   33

THE FENDER STORY *by Walter Carter*   40

ROCK & POP GUITARS *by Charles Shaar Murray*   44

BEATLE GUITARS *by Tony Bacon*   50

COUNTRY GUITARS *by Thomas Goldsmith*   58

JAPANESE GUITARS *by Hiroyuki Noguchi*   64

BLUES & SOUL GUITARS *by Paul Trynka*   70

RECORDING *by John Morrish*   77

INDEX   84

ACKNOWLEDGEMENTS   88

Britain was the base for the guitar-fuelled beat group boom of the 1960s. Here, XTC guitarist Dave Gregory offers an insider's view of the decade.

By the dawn of the 1960s the guitar had become the must-have accessory for all British teenage boys with fire in their bellies and rhythm in their bones. Few would be capable of mastering more than a handful of basic chords, but back then little more was necessary. The pop songs of the day were undemanding in content, unsophisticated in composition. The guitar not only provided the perfect accompaniment to the singing voice, but lent the player a certain romantic intrigue into the bargain.

At the same time, America's rock'n'roll boom was a far more serious affair. Its effect was slowly but surely filtering through to the UK with hit records by Elvis Presley, Buddy Holly, Ricky Nelson, The Everly Brothers and Duane Eddy, to name but a few. At the heart of these songs, to a greater or lesser degree, was an electric guitar. As a result, guitar students soon began seeking ways to 'electrify' their acoustic archtops and Spanish guitars, sometimes attaching crude magnetic pickups to their instruments, often wired optimistically through father's radio set. British youth was finding its voice too, even if it was a little croaky.

HANK MARVIN sports specs and Strat in Shads, '63-style.

Not until 1958 had a British company produced an amplifier equal to the task of flattering the sound of these primitive electric guitars and broadcasting it at a level compatible for use among drum kits and brass instruments. The Vox AC-15, all 15 watts of it, had become the first purpose-built guitar amplifier in the UK.

By 1960 Cliff Richard and The Shadows were the nation's pop darlings. While the girls screamed, the boys were spellbound by The Shadows' leader, guitarist Hank B. Marvin. He'd borrowed Buddy Holly's image wholesale, recently completing the ensemble with a brand new Fender Stratocaster guitar... just like Buddy's, but in a glamorous red finish. Specially imported from the US by his boss Cliff, Hank's Strat was the first of its type in the country, and bore little resemblance visually or sonically to anything currently available in England. It would play a large part in transforming its handler into the first British Guitar Hero before the year was out.

Hank was special because he could actually play the guitar properly, at a time when few English rock'n'rollers could. He used his Stratocaster, a Meazzi echo unit, and a newly-acquired Vox AC-30 Twin amplifier. This was double the power of the AC-15 and had been specially commissioned by The Shadows to cope with the larger theatres they were now playing. With this set-up Hank produced a warm, clear sound coloured further by his deft use of the Strat's 'Synchronized Tremolo' vibrato system. Together with tape echo and reverb, as well as another feature of the Vox amplifiers, valve tremolo, which added a throbbing pulse to the sound of the guitar, this was virtually the full range of effects, or gimmicks, available to electric guitarists in the early 1960s. But then the instrument itself was still a novelty. It would be some years before it was taken seriously as a credible musical force.

In June 1960 Johnny Kidd & The Pirates entered the UK charts with 'Shakin All Over', arguably the first bona fide home-grown British rock'n'roll hit of the decade. The record created quite a stir among guitar nuts, its chiming hook complemented by a simple staccato bass-and-guitar riff three octaves apart. Each chorus was launched with a solo E-minor triad, guitarist Joe Moretti frantically jerking the instrument's tremolo arm. Quivers down the backbone! The record raced to number two in Britain.

Within a month The Shadows scored their first solo number one UK hit with an instrumental tune called 'Apache'. It sold a million copies and, consequently, almost as many electric guitars. Simple in construction, its tune fitted perfectly the drums/bass/rhythm-guitar/lead-guitar format that constituted the standard group line-up of the day. Youth clubs and village halls up and down Britain throbbed to the sounds of would-be Pirates and Hank-alikes negotiating their way around their heroes' tunes. Wild, cool, but most importantly easy to play, these two records did more than most to instigate a national craze among the young to form beat groups, giving birth to what would eventually become a massive industry as demand snowballed for modern musical equipment.

Despite the continuing growth of the pop business, few real advances had been made since the 1950s either in songwriting, recording or playing standards. The Beatles arrived and changed everything. Not because they were particularly gifted as instrumentalists – indeed, they were a league or two below The Shadows in that respect – but because they played and sang their own brilliantly innovative songs with a joyful, energetic exuberance never before heard in a British group. Their second single 'Please Please Me' shot into the UK charts in the freezing January of 1963 and heralded the arrival of the first significant British musical trend of the 1960s, Merseybeat. A slew of talented groups and singers, mainly from The Beatles' home town of Liverpool in the north of England, would light up the charts in the coming year with inventive new songs performed with a refreshing vigour and vitality.

To be fair, Merseybeat did little to advance the technical standards of guitar playing, other than to instil a more dynamic and energetic attitude in the delivery. The Beatles' songs, on the other hand, introduced a whole new way of thinking in terms of chord structures. Suddenly every group wanted to write their own songs, which would involve a greater knowledge of chord shapes, inversions and progressions. Lennon and McCartney were constantly tossing in exotic-sounding chords such as sixths, major sevenths, augmenteds and diminisheds, many of which were a far cry from the standard three- and four-chord tricks around which most pop tunes had hitherto been based.

Meanwhile, something else was stirring in the south of England. With the country now firmly in the grip of Beatlemania, potential rivals had sprung from the London suburbs. An underground R&B band, The Rolling Stones, were making serious waves in the pubs and clubs of the metropolis and home counties with their gritty alternative to mop-top pop. Where The Beatles' music had its roots in everything from Carl Perkins and Gene Vincent through Little Richard to Buddy Holly and Roy Orbison, the Stones' influences included Muddy Waters, Howlin' Wolf, Jimmy Reed, Bo Diddley and Chuck Berry – American R&B acts and Chicago blues artists whose basic sound was built on raw, unpolished guitar playing.

Ironically, it would take a Beatle song to break the Stones. In October 1963 they covered a track specially written for them by Lennon and McCartney, 'I Wanna Be Your Man'. With loud, crudely-recorded, distorted guitars, incorporating a searing solo executed with a bottle-neck slide (the first on a UK single), the record gatecrashed the UK Top 20 at the end of November. British R&B had arrived. Youngsters everywhere were thrilled. Parents were suitably annoyed.

The Rolling Stones continued to gather momentum during 1964 thanks to some dynamic singles and a tremendous debut

THE SHADOWS' first album, 1961, with borrowed Tele and (just visible) that red Strat.

SHEET MUSIC for She Loves You inexplicably came in the guitar-unfriendly key of E-flat.

LP that crystalised the current state of alternative British pop as hard-edged R&B with a heavy beat and an arrogant swagger. Guitars were mixed well to the fore, and the record celebrated Keith Richards' love of Chuck Berry's playing, a bluesy, rocking style characterised by much string-bending. This involved pushing the strings sideways, across the fret, to alter the pitch – no mean feat as the strings of the day were comparatively heavy-gauged, often with a wound G, sometimes wrapped with distinctly player-unfriendly plastic tape. Even so, aspiring soloists realised that, once mastered, this technique could add much excitement to a performance, particularly if the amplifier was overdriven slightly to distort the sound.

The Beatles returned to the UK from their first triumphant US visit in late February 1964 and brought with them an important new element to their sound. George Harrison had taken delivery of a new electric 12-string guitar from the Rickenbacker company. While not the first electric 12 ever

arresting arpeggiated solo guitar introduction that traced a brooding Am/C/D/F/Am/E/Am chord sequence. The intricacies of the performance were dissected by guitar students the world over. A little more difficult than the usual faux-Chuck Berry double-stops and reckless neck mangling, this called for a degree of accuracy with the picking hand. If you could hack it, you'd arrived! Even today the riff still occupies a place, somewhere around stage three, in the great 12-Step Master-The-Guitar programme.

The following month, Dave Berry released 'The Crying Game' which featured a guitar effect that many still believe to be an early example of wah-wah. In fact, the 'crying' effect was created with a footpedal dating from the late 1950s. Manufactured by Rowe Industries in the US, the DeArmond Volume & Tone pedal would rock vertically to raise or lower the volume, and from side to side to alter the tone. Neat footwork combining both effects could pay extraordinary

LIVERPOOL 1964: the sheer joy of being in a pop group.

produced, it was nonetheless only the second or third of its type made by Rickenbacker and had a unique sound – almost like a blend of harpsichord, guitar and piano. Its lower four strings were paired with a second set tuned one octave higher, while the top E and B strings were doubled in unison – standard stringing for 12-string guitars, except that the heavier of the octave pairs was on the 'top', not the 'bottom' (from the player's view). The group featured it on their new single 'Can't Buy Me Love', but it was the b-side, 'You Can't Do That', which really demonstrated what the guitar could do. The Beatles then started work on their first feature film, *A Hard Day's Night*, which showcased the Rickenbacker extensively, both visually and on the soundtrack. The opening multitracked Dm7sus4 chord of the title song effectively pronounced that a brand new voice, born of the 1960s, had arrived in the universe of the guitar.

More notable guitar hooks would drift across the ether during the British summer of 1964. The Animals, from Newcastle in north-east England, delivered the first six-minute single in June and sent it straight to number one in the UK charts, repeating that feat three months later in the US. Undoubtedly what sold 'The House Of The Rising Sun' was an

dividends – Chet Atkins had used it to great effect on his 1960 LP *Teensville* – although the casualty rate due to muscular cramps is not recorded.

Another striking sound assaulted the British charts in August 1964 (and three months later in the US). The Kinks, a teenage R&B outfit from Muswell Hill, north London, released their own song 'You Really Got Me'. Beginning with a dry, rasping guitar chopping out a two-chord riff, the song built to a cacophonous frenzy, exploding into an incendiary solo from the 17-year-old guitarist Dave Davies. Possibly inspired by Keith Richards' sound on the recent Rolling Stones UK hit 'It's All Over Now', but without the reverb, Davies had used a similar guitar to Keith's – a mid-priced Harmony Meteor – through a tiny Elpico amplifier, the loudspeaker of which he'd slashed with a blade to add more distortion to the sound. The song is often credited as being "the first heavy rock riff ever" – usually by The Kinks themselves – but it certainly set a new benchmark for guitar soloing and helped consolidate the electric guitar's increasing influence on the music scene.

ANIMALS guitarist Hilton Valentine was the man with the arpeggios to imitate in 1964.

From the same club circuit that spawned The Rolling Stones emerged The Yardbirds. Though not destined to be as successful, they nonetheless would prove integral to the continuing development of English pop in general and guitar playing in particular. The group had a gifted young guitarist, Eric Clapton, whose reputation among the hip cognoscenti was rapidly spreading. Clapton's hero was Buddy Holly, but he'd become hooked on the blues after hearing a Big Bill Broonzy record that had somehow found its way on to a BBC radio request programme. The Yardbirds' first single, 'I Wish You Would', was released in June 1964; it was backed with 'A Certain Girl', which displayed Clapton's prodigious talent as a soloist. His legato phrasing was strident, confident and eloquent, and together with some elegant note-bending created a perfectly woven solo, revealing an intelligence and musicianship that belied Clapton's 18 years. To colour the tone of the guitar he'd used a device that artificially distorted the sound: a fuzz box, or distortion pedal.

THE KINKS put the riff in pop.

The earliest distortion units had been developed in the US by the Gibson company in 1962 as an optional built-in effect to their solidbody EB-0 bass guitar. Called, appropriately enough, Fuzztone, it would also be incorporated into their new custom-order-only EBSF-1250, a huge solid guitar with two necks, one for bass, the other a regular six-string. As few guitarists had need of such instruments, the company soon offered the Fuzztone unit in a separate battery-operated pedal and called it the Maestro. The problem with the Maestro was that, although it produced a novel crackling effect, there was insufficient gain running into it from the guitar to produce any sustain, resulting in the distorted sound cutting off after a few moments. It was the British session guitarist Vic Flick, of The John Barry Seven, who took the problem to Gary Hurst, a young electronics engineer. Hurst set about designing a unit similar to the Gibson pedal but with the required energy necessary to hold a note reasonably efficiently. His improved design, marketed as the Tone Bender, was one of the first effects pedals on the market in Britain, starting a trend for sound gadgets that would be central to the evolving sound of the electric guitar as the decade progressed.

MAESTRO have a fuzzbox and everyone's going to abuse it.

The burgeoning British R&B scene would produce more significant guitar talent during 1965. In February, The Who made their chart debut with 'I Can't Explain', a thinly disguised rewrite of The Kinks' second hit, 'All Day And All Of The Night', but with a taut, jabbing Rickenbacker 12-string playing the irresistible three-chord riff. It was written and played by their leader Pete Townshend who, while perhaps not as accomplished a soloist as some of his contemporaries, had nonetheless forged a remarkable style based on feedback and heavy, thrashing chords. Feedback is the electronic howling and squealing that occurs when the sound from the amplifier feeds back into the pickups of the guitar.

In the past feedback, like distortion, had been a nuisance, something to be avoided at all costs. But with music now increasing in volume and energy it was yet another exciting element that could be used to great effect under the right circumstances. For The Who's next release, 'Anyway, Anyhow, Anywhere', Townshend turned in a solo that made the most of this sonic aberration. He hit hard chords through a loud amplifier while turning his guitar to face the loudspeakers. Rolling the tone control of the neck-position pickup of his Rickenbacker back to zero, and soloing on the brighter bridge pickup (the one most sensitive to feedback), he could make-and-break the piercing signal by toggling the pickup selector switch back and forth rhythmically.

Feedback and other not-entirely-musical approaches to

playing would often lead to the destruction of the volatile Who's stage equipment when they performed live, the intensity of the noise mounting to a horrendous climax from which there was no other way down. Maximum R&B indeed! But The Who's performances, both on-stage and in the studio, depended as much on sheer volume as they did on adolescent frustration. Before 1965 was over the group would deliver their epochal anthem, 'My Generation'. Louder, wilder and more exciting than anything that had preceded it, the recording packed a pounding two-chord riff, a gloriously sneering vocal, a ground-breaking bass guitar solo and a blur of thrashing drums and feedback guitar. The spectre of heavy rock was already looming.

By contrast, 1965 was also the year of folk-rock. Bob Dylan's new album *Bringing It All Back Home* had been recorded with an electric band. When he played at the Newport Folk Festival in the US that July he took to the stage with Paul Butterfield's Blues Band in tow, and strapped on a Fender Stratocaster. Opinion is divided as to whether the frosty reception afforded him by the assembled folkies that night was due to his electric guitar, or the fact that he'd only performed three songs. One thing was clear: the lonesome troubadour with the acoustic guitar was ready to rock.

A month earlier The Byrds had appeared from America's west coast with an electric reworking of a recent Dylan song, 'Mr Tambourine Man'. Folk guitarists Jim (later Roger) McGuinn, Gene Clark and David Crosby had been so impressed by The Beatles' movie *A Hard Day's Night* the previous summer they'd decided to form a pop group straight away. Inspired by George Harrison's sound, McGuinn immediately purchased a Rickenbacker 12-string electric. It was, he discovered, a difficult instrument to play, but McGuinn's somewhat fumbling style nevertheless created a magical sonic foil to his group's sublime three-part vocal harmonies, a blend previously only hinted at by Britain's Searchers during the Merseybeat period. McGuinn's jangling guitar would dominate The Byrds' records for at least the next three years, and is today still considered to be the classic sound of the electric 12-string.

In England, however, the folk scene had scarcely dared venture beyond the pubs and coffee bars. Since The Springfields had broken up, only Donovan had made any commercial impact in recent years, his 'Catch The Wind' earning him a reputation as the teenage British Bob Dylan surrogate. Martin Carthy was the unofficial godfather of English folk guitar, a peerless traditional acoustic player who had championed the young Paul Simon during his first visit to the UK as an unknown in the early 1960s. When Simon returned to the US he took with him Carthy's arrangement of 'Scarborough Fair' and later, with his singing partner Art Garfunkel, turned it (uncredited) into a huge American hit, an event not lost on the hard-working Carthy. Bert Jansch and John Renbourn were two more luminaries from the same background who also remained faithful to their acoustic instruments, thus eluding mass recognition. Jansch's version of Davey Graham's tune 'Angie' had been the British fingerstyle player's entrance examination piece for several years; his 1966 album *Jack Orion* would include a tune called 'Blackwater Side' which would leave a huge impression on a young session guitarist and future legend called Jimmy Page.

Eric Clapton had quit The Yardbirds early in 1965, the call of the blues pulling him further from the group's aspirations to commercial success, and he'd joined John Mayall's Bluesbreakers. Mayall was an uncompromising blues purist who had been quick to recognise Eric's potential. He offered

PETE TOWNSHEND armed with a lethal Rickenbacker.

McGUINN and jangly Rick.

Clapton a small room in his house, and the guitarist moved in. Immersing himself in Mayall's vast collection of rare American blues records, Clapton crammed his head with the music of B.B., Albert and Freddy King, Otis Rush, Buddy Guy, and their Chicago-based brethren.

On seeing the sleeve of Freddy King's 1961 LP *Let's Hide Away And Dance Away*, in which King is posed with an early 1950s Gibson Les Paul gold-top guitar, Clapton headed straight for London's music shop district in and around the Charing Cross Road, in search of a similar model. Clapton found a later version of the instrument, with a sunburst top and improved 'humbucking' pickups, manufactured in the late 1950s. These original-design Les Paul guitars had at that time been out of production for four or five years.

LONDON's West End music shops, 1964: happy hunting ground for would-be groups.

This seminal pairing of player and instrument would eventually lead to a revolution in history, and change forever the attitudes of players and audiences the world over. As the summer progressed, Clapton continued his single-minded pursuit of his style, building on the foundations laid by his Chicago heroes. The unique tone and long, natural sustain he'd discovered in the Les Paul guitar was sweetened further by an exemplary left-hand vibrato, which added an eloquent authority to the new musical language he was exploring.

String-bending was by now a firmly established technique among guitarists, many of whom had discovered it could be achieved a lot easier by 'slack-stringing' their instruments. This involved discarding the low E-string, moving the remaining five one notch upwards, and tuning the top E down to B, the B down to G, and so on. The top E would be replaced by a thin banjo A which could be purchased separately. By using this method, players could bend their now-lighter strings through as much as a tone and a half if necessary, depending on how far they scaled the fingerboard. It was also easier to add vibrato with the left hand, as some of the more adept Chicago bluesmen had done. By gently rotating the wrist, the string could be 'pushed and pulled' repeatedly across the fret, creating a more human tone and even adding to the note's sustain. This difficult technique, once perfected, was far more musical than the tremolo-arm method, enhancing the expression of notes and phrases and lending the more accomplished player a musicianly credibility. Vibrato soon became the latest trick to master.

Eric Clapton's place in The Yardbirds had been filled by another guitar genius from the Surrey area in south-east England, one Jeff Beck. On arriving at the studio to record their first single with Beck (Graham Gouldman's 'Heart Full Of Soul') the band discovered that their manager and producer, Giorgio Gomelsky, had hired two Indian musicians to play on the session – a tabla player and a sitar player. The opening riff to the song did emote a very Indian flavour, but the delicate sound of the sitar was not dynamic enough to carry the necessary impact that the track demanded. It was therefore down to the new guitarist to imitate the sound and playing style of the Indian instrument, which he did with a Fender Telecaster played through a Tone Bender fuzz pedal borrowed from his friend Jimmy Page. In so doing, Beck accidentally created the first example of another new style, one that would come to be known as psychedelia. Coined in allusion to the latest drug fashion to hit the US, the hallucinogenic LSD, the term when applied to music suggested an altered mind-state that might be realised – under its influence – by swirling, reverb-drenched, fuzz-tone guitars, often borrowing phrases and riffs from Indian scales. This novel effect would soon catch on in a big way.

By the year's end, two of the biggest-selling records in the UK would feature fuzz guitar: The Rolling Stones'

'Satisfaction', and 'Keep On Running' by The Spencer Davis Group. Even the mighty Beatles had made use of fuzz on their ground-breaking *Rubber Soul* LP, for Paul McCartney's bass part on 'Think For Yourself'. Although none of these songs could be considered remotely psychedelic, the new sound had nonetheless established itself in the minds of both musicians and the record-buying public alike. The gadgets began selling and a number of similar products soon found their way onto the market.

The inclusion of a real sitar on The Beatles' *Rubber Soul* album inspired a popular curiosity in Indian music, and all manner of Eastern instruments would pepper many a recording over the next couple of years. The Yardbirds continued a quest for exotic textures. Their ambitious 'Shapes Of Things' shot into the UK Top Five in February 1966, its abstract message borne on a marching two-chord guitar motif, breaking into double-tempo for Jeff Beck's awesome solo where his guitar assumes the guise of some psychedelically deranged gypsy violin. 'Over, Under, Sideways, Down' followed in May, taking another Indian-flavoured guitar hook into both UK and US charts. Untouchable in his field, the ever-inventive Beck had become Player Of The Moment.

The now massively successful Rolling Stones had temporarily abandoned their R&B roots with the spring release of the *Aftermath* album. Brian Jones' use of the sitar, both on the album and the single 'Paint It Black', was a brave departure from the tried and tested formula, and signalled real progress and a need to develop. The Beatles had begun experimenting with the studio's tape machines, slowing some tracks down, playing others backwards, all in a search for ever more weird sounds. One of the new psychedelic groups, The Creation, boasted an innovative guitarist called Eddie Phillips who, in addition to some fine pioneering work with feedback, had also been the first to apply a violin bow to his instrument. It was a period of great change, and of endless possibilities.

The recording of John Mayall's *Blues Breakers With Eric Clapton* album in April 1966 marked another watershed in the changing sound of the electric guitar.

EDDIE PHILLIPS of The Creation in 1966 deploying an avant-Page violin bow.

Having abandoned the use of the fuzz pedal after his initial Yardbirds recordings, Clapton discovered the perfect sound for the music he was playing with Mayall: the Gibson Les Paul hooked up to a 50-watt Marshall combo amplifier. By increasing the volume on the amp to a magical 'sweet spot', the guitar would overload it naturally, creating a smooth, more musical distortion. This did incur a problem in the studio, where engineer Gus Dudgeon experienced some difficulty in preventing the sound from bouncing around the room and into the drum and vocal microphones. Recording a rehearsal, Dudgeon and producer Mike Vernon invited the guitarist into the control room to demonstrate the problem to him. On hearing the playback, Clapton was ecstatic. "That's the sound I'm looking for!" he exclaimed. "Don't change a thing!"

The finished product probably remains the greatest white blues album of all time. Through his use of overdrive distortion, controlled feedback and vibrato, Clapton had set new goals for aspiring guitarists, regardless of their chosen style. But when it was released in July, *Blues Breakers*, for all its peerless attributes, was something of an anachronism compared with what was happening on the current music scene. Certainly there were enough hardcore blues guitar fanatics around to hike the record into the UK album charts, but Clapton, having grown restless, had already left Mayall's group in search of new pastures. He'd teamed up with two new colleagues, drummer Ginger Baker and bassist Jack Bruce, to form what would become the first heavy rock group, Cream.

Fresh Cream, the group's debut album, caused much excitement on its release at the end of 1966. Baker and Bruce, though both veterans of the R&B scene, also had strong backgrounds in jazz. Both were fiery in temperament, and this reflected itself in their often ferocious playing, providing Clapton with a huge, powerful engine with which to drive his exquisite, improvised excursions. The group had upgraded their equipment to the new 100-watt Marshall amplifiers, and Baker had doubled the size of his drum kit. Listening to the album it was sometimes hard to believe that three musicians could create such an enormous sound.

Cream's single, 'I Feel Free', was issued at the same time as the album, and Clapton's solo delivered a sound more akin to a wind instrument than a guitar. Nothing like it had ever been heard. Clapton himself later described it as his 'woman tone'. "It's a sweet sound," he would tell *Beat Instrumental* magazine six months later, "more like the human voice than a guitar... it calls for the correct use of distortion." In fact, by rolling the tone control of the neck pickup of his Gibson back to zero and playing at high volume through the powerful Marshall, no fuzz pedals were necessary. The extraordinary effect also demonstrated how the new amplifier designs were helping to inspire the rapidly expanding vocabulary of contemporary music.

JIMI prepares to bombard an expectant Marquee audience.

No sooner had Cream rewritten the book of rock guitar than Jimi Hendrix arrived from the US and tore it up completely. Throughout 1967 and 1968 he reinvented the sound of the instrument time and time again, expanding its horizons, presenting undreamed sonic possibilities, and bringing the blues into the nuclear age. 'Stone Free', the b-side of his first single 'Hey Joe' (released in December 1966), provided the first evidence of the incredible prowess of Hendrix, who played left-handed yet operated on a normal Fender Stratocaster restrung and turned upside down. On 'Stone Free' he played a heavily overdriven guitar solo, spitting out a blistering scatter of notes, the Strat's tremolo arm wrenched to near breaking point. It was a staggering performance, despatched with sheer adrenalin-rush abandon. The song faded with its final chord mutating into a ludicrously distorted, wildly undulating low F as the instrument's bridge hardware was brutally abused by its master. This was light-years from 'Apache'!

The release of his debut album, *Are You Experienced*, in the spring of 1967 confirmed beyond question the genius of Hendrix. Thirty years on, few guitarists have come close to matching his sound or can approach the depth of feeling which underscored his work. That he would all but burn out within two years was, perhaps, inevitable. *Are You Experienced* and the two albums that followed – *Axis: Bold As Love* and *Electric Ladyland* – still stand as the decade's creative high points in guitar-based rock. By 1969, under intolerable pressure to tour, write, record... and tour some more, Hendrix could produce little to compare with his astonishing achievements on those early albums where he had embraced many musical styles. He ranged effortlessly from simple two-minute pop songs to grand psychedelic masterpieces, through funky soul tunes to heavy riff rock, all forged from a rich seam of the deepest, darkest blues.

Much apocrypha has come to light concerning Jimi's uncanny insight and mythical gifts, one for example claiming that he instinctively knew exactly how a solo would sound when recorded backwards. Yet one only has to hear the

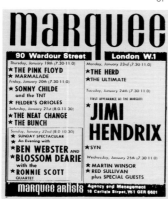

JIMI HENDRIX and Pink Floyd in one week at London's Marquee Club in 1967.

reverse-track solo on the title song of his first album to appreciate that miracles were indeed possible, that somewhere a god exists. Hendrix's legacy is more widely felt today than it was during his brief lifetime, and this is testament to his phenomenal gift: that of a blues musician with a universal message, delivered with a showman's swagger, the whole blessed – or cursed – with a poet's heart and a seemingly limitless imagination.

Always underrated as a rhythm guitarist, Hendrix had a style that owed much to his early apprenticeship backing the likes of Little Richard and The Isley Brothers on lengthy one-nighter tours of the States in the early 1960s. These were acts specialising in energetic dance music where the guitarist was very much the sideman, his function to provide a solid rhythmic foundation in tandem with the bass and the drums. From this tradition came the Tamla Motown organisation of Detroit, a phenomenally successful outfit during the 1960s, producing hit after dance hit by a variety of black artists, all backed by the same coterie of writers and studio musicians on whom their success depended. Strangely, few people knew – or cared – who these faceless geniuses were. After all, they were simply doing a job in providing backing tracks for stars like The Supremes or The Four Tops, and there would be no ostentatious solo flights on their records. Even so, Robert White, Joe Messina, Eddie Willis and Marv Tarplin, to name but a few, were all brilliant guitarists who knew their place in the Motown studio, unsung heroes happy to do the job for which they were paid, but with little or no recognition. Their real contribution would eventually be acknowledged in the next decade as the funk phenomenon took hold.

Another American guitarist gaining popularity with his minimal, brittle yet deeply soulful style was Steve Cropper. The studio guitarist at Stax Records in Memphis, he was also a member of Booker T & The MGs who scored a huge US hit in 1962 with 'Green Onions', a simple 12-bar instrumental with an infectious, easy-to-master guitar hook. Cropper had gone on to write and record with such soul legends as Aretha Franklin, Otis Redding, Sam & Dave, Wilson Pickett and Eddie Floyd, as well as creating many legendary tracks with the MGs. Yet his style remained the complete antithesis of much of what was currently in vogue, his Telecaster producing clean, precise, economical chords and phrases that never once upstaged the vocalist, always finding the perfect riff for the perfect moment. Never using two notes where one would do, Cropper remains the master of the less-is-more school of musical thought, his contribution to the progress of guitar playing every bit as valid as those who played twice as many notes, twice as loud and at twice the speed.

Manufacturers would continue to keep pace with the ever-changing fads of musicians as more and more experimental playing styles continued to evolve into the latter half of the 1960s. Light-gauge, wire-wound strings had been available for some time, and it was now possible for players to create their own custom-gauge set of strings to suit their individual playing style. Jimi Hendrix hit upon the idea of tuning his guitar down by approximately one semitone. This not only made string-bending easier, as the tension was decreased, but fortuitously gave his Stratocaster a more mellow midrange tone quality, which became central to his unique sound. Hendrix, like Cream, endorsed the use of the popular Marshall 'stack' – a 100-watt amplifier perched atop two

NEW HORIZONS in sound as Roger plays a solo on the wah-wah trousers.

speaker cabinets, each of which housed four 12" speakers. The imposing edifice not only looked very impressive but delivered an incredibly powerful sound.

In the spring of 1967, Vox launched an important new effect pedal, the wah-wah. It had been designed by an American engineer called Stan Cutler who worked for Warwick Industries, owners of the Thomas Organ company in the States who had a controlling interest in Vox in the UK. Cutler had been working on a system for amplifying brass instruments in big bands, utilising his 'Ampliphonic' music stand, a unit with a built-in effects pre-amp. One of the effects was intended to simulate the sound of a muted trumpet "in the style of Clyde McCoy". Inevitably, somebody in the R&D department played a guitar through it and decided it could be more practically employed built into a pedal accessory, for use with any instrument. Previously, the DeArmond volume/tone pedal had been effective in merely removing high frequencies from the signal passing through it, as does the tone control on a guitar. But the wah-wah actually boosted the harmonic peaks of the many midrange frequencies as the pedal was rocked up and down.

The Vox wah-wah pedal proved a remarkable success, its first use on record being Cream's 'Tales Of Brave Ulysses', released as the b-side to their single 'Strange Brew' in May 1967. While recording tracks for Cream's second album in New York during April, Eric Clapton had paid a visit to Manny's music store on 48th Street and, out of curiosity, had picked up one of the new devices. Anxious to keep one step ahead of the mercurial Hendrix who was rapidly stealing much of his thunder, Clapton used the pedal to devastating effect on the track which remains as one of his most exciting performances. Hendrix soon followed suit, his wah-wah-powered 'Burning Of The Midnight Lamp' being the first British Top 20 hit to feature the sound, in August 1967. The wah-wah would remain an essential part of Jimi's musical arsenal until his death in 1970.

Throughout 1967, the year of flower power and the summer of love, musical experimentation continued unabated, providing a colourful sonic counterpoint to the outlandish fashion scene that had propagated through the boutiques of London's Carnaby Street. The Beatles' new album, *Sgt Pepper's Lonely Hearts Club Band*, and the world anthem single that followed it, 'All You Need Is Love', had the group playing still more oddly distorted guitars; 'Lucy In The Sky With Diamonds' featured a Leslie rotating speaker, normally used to amplify the Hammond organ but here providing a different vibrato-like chorus effect for guitar.

The Pink Floyd, a new group from Cambridge in England, released their first album in July 1967, guitarist Syd Barrett using his Fender Esquire more as a sound effects unit than a musical instrument. His use of bottleneck slide through fuzz, echo and reverb positively redefined the psychedelic blueprint. Even the great white god of the blues guitar, Eric Clapton, had permed his hair and taken to playing a frivolously decorated Gibson SG, done out in the gaudy dayglo colours of the day by Dutch pop artists The Fool.

Sitars were everywhere. Later in 1967 the Danelectro company would invent an electric guitar that could imitate the sound of that most awkward-to-master Indian instrument. Called the Coral Sitar, it was designed by studio guitarist Vinnie Bell, and actually included a separate set of 13 'drone' strings. First into the charts with it were The Lemon Pipers with 'Green Tambourine', a number one hit in the US at the end of the year.

PETER GREEN with Les Paul.

These colourful new clothes did not, unfortunately, have a long shelf life. Neither did they fit perfectly all who wore them. The Rolling Stones' answer to *Sgt Pepper* was *Their Satanic Majesties Request*. It arrived in time for Christmas but was greeted, somewhat unfairly in retrospect, with a giant raspberry from fans and critics alike. Even The Beatles' self-produced TV movie, *Magical Mystery Tour*, screened in the UK just after Christmas, seemed to celebrate the basic silliness of the Flower Power phenomenon. Spoilsports the world over predicted the end of the hippie movement and even of The Beatles as a group. But the jetsam of the psychedelic period would clear as the new year of 1968 arrived, making way for a more serious approach to music and guitar playing. The British Blues Boom was about to begin.

Eric Clapton had been replaced in John Mayall's Bluesbreakers by yet another soon-to-be-legendary figure, Peter Green. *A Hard Road*, Mayall's 1967 album which featured Green, revealed the new guitarist attempting to clone his illustrious predecessor, with varying degrees of success. After less than a year in the group he'd left to form his own band, Fleetwood Mac. Their debut LP, released in February 1968, showcased Green's blossoming talent, not only as guitarist but as vocalist and harmonica player too. But it was his soulful guitar style that stood out above all else. Using a 1959 Gibson Les Paul, Green had avoided the huge, overdriven Marshall sound favoured by Clapton and Hendrix in favour of a cleaner, sweetly cutting tone. At some point the neck-position pickup of his guitar had inadvertently been reinstalled wrongly, which meant that when both pickups were activated simultaneously they were 'out of phase'. This produced a hollowed quality to the sound that perfectly complemented Green's sad, plaintive playing style. The understated nature of his playing, free of effects or treatments of any kind, meant that his solos never outstayed their welcome. Always delivered straight from the heart, they were perfectly executed, passionate statements that always left audiences wanting more.

Some remarkable fresh talents came to light on the so-called 'underground' scene as 1968 progressed. Peter Green's replacement in the Bluesbreakers was Mick Taylor, a 17-year-old guitarist from Hatfield, just north of London. As sensitive and technically skilled a blues player as ever emerged from the era, Taylor would eventually plunge down-market to find fame and fortune in The Rolling Stones in 1969. Green himself added another prodigious young player to his group in 18-year-old Danny Kirwan, giving Fleetwood Mac an unbeatable twin lead guitar format, alongside their talented slide guitarist Jeremy Spencer. By the year's end they would score a huge UK number one hit with the Shadows-influenced instrumental 'Albatross'. Another group from the London blues scene, Free, included 18-year-old Paul Kossoff, who took Eric Clapton's 'woman tone', added a wide, shrill, left-handed vibrato, and thus helped gain his band near legendary status by the end of the decade.

Exactly why this ethnic blues music, indigenous to black Americans in the Mississippi Delta and the Chicago ghettos, should have been expressed most effectively by middle-class, teenage, British white boys is one of life's imponderables. Nonetheless, it had clearly struck a very sensitive nerve in the souls of countless young musicians and music fans.

JIMMY PAGE with Les Paul.

The extraordinary success of Cream and Jimi Hendrix provoked a new attitude among many players. No longer content simply to be group members, they now aspired to being featured soloists. Just as The Beatles had inspired a nation of wannabe-songwriters, so Cream's example led to a legion of Clapton copyists who often self-indulgently chased their dreams by wallowing in extended workouts. 'Songs' merely served as vehicles for these lengthy, often tedious blues guitar solos.

A few maverick spirits broke from the pack. Steve Howe, guitarist with Keith West's Tomorrow, had found his voice in a thoroughly unfashionable Gibson ES-175D archtop, ostensibly a jazz guitar — yet in his hands the instrument was perfectly at home with Tomorow's hippie psych/pop inclinations. Howe's clean, bright sound and impeccable technique set him apart from his peers, and he remained true to his original blueprint well into the future, eventually finding huge success in the 1970s with Yes. Alvin Lee, from Nottingham in the north of England, fronted Ten Years After and proved to be the fastest player on the block. His group's live album, *Undead*, set new technical goals for guitarists and frightened the pants off many a hopeful pretender. And from south Wales, Dave Edmunds' Love Sculpture released a five-minute guitar arrangement of Khachaturian's 'Sabre Dance' which had heads turning and jaws dropping as the 45 tore up the British singles charts in December 1968.

Folk music finally took a brave step into the rock arena as Fairport Convention put drums and the sublime electric guitar of Richard Thompson into traditional-sounding English songs, a style that Fairport would successfully develop with skill and taste into the next decade. In the US it was The Band, who advanced their own traditional course with their debut *Music From Big Pink*, featuring four original compositions from their gifted guitarist Robbie Robertson. *Big Pink* left a profound influence on Eric Clapton, who had just been described by *Rolling Stone* magazine as "the master of the cliché". Listening to Robertson's clean, simple playing, Clapton decided he'd had enough of Cream, and the group played its final concert at the end of November 1968. It had been the year of the Guitar Hero... and now it seemed as if there were hundreds to choose from.

Also in 1968, the Les Paul guitar had been reintroduced by Gibson, who had finally acceded to public demand by issuing two 'replicas' of 1950s models: a 1955-style gold-top, now called the Standard, and a black Custom with gold-plated metal parts and humbucking pickups. Though faithful to the original designs, they sadly lacked the magical tonal properties that had made the originals so special. Nonetheless they sold like hot cakes, despite a hefty price tag, and have been in virtually unbroken production ever since.

In 1969 pop music finally lost its innocence, and rock entered its gawky adolescence. Seeded in the American rock'n'roll of the 1950s, gestating for a decade on a diet of urban Chicago blues and Merseybeat, nursed and nurtured at various points along the way by the caring midwifery of Alexis Korner, John Mayall, Giorgio Gomelsky and British blues champion/producer Mike Vernon, the child would make its mark on the world in the early spring with an astonishing debut from a brand new group, Led Zeppelin.

Jimmy Page had entered the world of the studio musician late in 1962 at the tender age of 18. His first session was playing rhythm guitar behind Jet Harris and Tony Meehan's 'Diamonds'. It was the duo's first single since leaving The

△ HÖFNER VERITHIN
Produced 1960-1965; this example c1961

During the 1950s Höfner of Germany had kept many European players supplied with decent, affordable guitars when American instruments were hard to get. As US guitars became more plentiful in the early 1960s, Höfner lost some of its individuality and competed more directly with American instruments. The Verithin, based on Gibson's Thinline series, was a staple among up-and-coming pop groups. This one belongs to Bert Weedon.

BERT WEEDON was a busy British session guitarist who also helped to popularise guitars through his regular appearances on children's TV shows. Weedon used Hofner's new narrow-body Verithin model in the early 1960s (right) until Guild built him a special "signature" model (see p.37).

JAZZ GUITARS

By the close of the 1950s the sound of the electric guitar was familiar in jazz, but few guitar players had band-leading ambitions. Most were content to play in the familiar trio or quartet format rather than place the guitar as a frontline instrument in a larger ensemble. However, during the 1960s the emergence of some major new guitarists would take the instrument to the forefront of jazz.

The complex bebop lines of guitarists Tal Farlow and Jimmy Raney, inspired by the harmonic intricacy of saxophonists like Charlie Parker, had become the benchmark for a generation of jazz guitarists in the 1950s. Johnny Smith had unveiled a lush, relaxed sound, Herb Ellis with the Oscar Peterson Trio had built on the work of Charlie Christian to create a hard-swinging bluesy style of jazz guitar, and Barney Kessel was the best-known and most popular jazz guitarist of the 1950s, in constant demand as an accompanist.

But jazz music had moved on. The major innovators by the late 1950s were saxophonists, trumpeters and pianists whose line-ups seldom featured the guitar, which did not really fit into the hard-bop style of Art Blakey's Jazz Messengers or the small groups of Miles Davis.

Stylistically, guitar players were slow to respond to the possibilities of the modal approach to jazz unveiled by the ever-questioning Davis on his seminal 1959 album *Kind Of Blue*. The guitar in jazz was certainly in the front pack, but not yet among the leaders. Soon that would change dramatically.

In September 1959 the jazz saxophonist Cannonball Adderley was playing a concert in Indianapolis, Indiana. Later in the evening he dropped into the Missile Club and took a seat

near the back. On stage a trio of guitar, organ and drums was playing a selection of jazz standards and originals. Within minutes Adderley had moved to the front row and sat right in front of the guitarist, Wes Montgomery, spellbound by the sheer brilliance of his playing.

Idea after idea poured out of Montgomery's Gibson L-5CES guitar, perfectly executed with precision even at fast tempos, even though he picked the strings with his right-hand thumb instead of the customary plectrum. Like a master story-teller, Montgomery kept Adderley's attention for chorus after chorus as he unravelled his tale and drew it to a satisfying conclusion. Starting his solos with single-line improvisation, he would shift up a gear by playing entire choruses in unison octaves, thickening the sound. To bring his solo to a climax, he'd outline fast-moving melodic lines with block chords, played on the upper strings of the guitar. The effect was stunning!

Back in New York, Adderley swept into the offices of Riverside Records in a state of excitement and persuaded producer Orrin Keepnews to go to Indianapolis to hear this master musician. On the same day Keepnews read a magazine article by composer and writer Gunther Schuller praising the guitarist, and off he set. Keepnews' journey echoed that of producer John Hammond two decades earlier, who went to Oklahoma City to hear electric guitar pioneer Charlie Christian (and Montgomery's primary inspiration), a trip that launched the innovative Christian's recording career.

Within three weeks Keepnews had recorded *The Wes Montgomery Trio* in New York. Although the album caught the attention of musicians, it received mixed reviews and sales were disappointing. Montgomery played well throughout, however, and his interpretation of Thelonious Monk's 'Round Midnight' is a masterpiece. For the guitarist's second Riverside

album, 1960's *The Incredible Jazz Guitar Of Wes Montgomery*, Keepnews teamed him with a top-flight New York rhythm section, and the result more than vindicated the album's title. Many sides of Montgomery's talent were on display here: his delicate treatment of a ballad ('Polka Dots And Moonbeams'), his breathtaking up-tempo soloing ('Airegin'), his skilful development of a solo over five or six minutes ('Gone With The Wind'), his mastery of the blues form ('D Natural Blues') and his ability to write memorable tunes ('West Coast Blues', 'Four On Six', 'Mister Walker'). This album was absolute confirmation that a major new jazz guitar voice had arrived.

From 1959 to 1964 Montgomery recorded 19 albums for Riverside and its subsidiary label Fantasy and regularly topped the annual *Down Beat* readers' and critics' polls. He was partnered on record with several leading jazz artists including vibraphonist Milt Jackson, organist Jimmy Smith and pianist George Shearing. An outstanding release from this period was *Full House*, recorded live at Tsubo's Coffee Shop in San Francisco in June 1962 with the saxophonist Johnny Griffin and the rhythm section from Miles Davis' group: Wynton Kelly (piano), Paul Chambers (bass) and Jimmy Cobb (drums). It includes a beautiful solo performance of the ballad 'I've Grown Accustomed To Her Face' which Montgomery played entirely solo in chord-melody style.

For his final Riverside album, *Fusion*, Montgomery was featured with a string orchestra under the direction of Jimmy Jones. This radical shift from the familiar jazz combo setting was too much for many jazz critics, who felt that the result lacked bite, but Montgomery himself regarded it as his best recording so far. Attractively recorded and with excellent

1960

WES MONTGOMERY was the greatest jazz guitarist of the 1960s. He had an instantly distinctive sound, due in part to using his thumb rather than a pick, and often featured fluid octave runs. Montgomery had signed to Riverside in 1959 at the age of 34 when he was at the hub of the thriving local jazz scene in Indianapolis, working with many excellent musicians including his brothers Buddy (piano/vibraphone) and Monk (the first jazz bassist to play the electric bass), with whom he recorded three albums. But it was this aptly-named 1960 album (left) that really established Montgomery as a guitarist of world-class quality.

△ GIBSON L-5CESN

Produced 1960-1969 (this style); this example July 1964

Jazz guitarists entered the 1960s with their conservative view of the instrument intact. Their electric guitar of choice was a large hollow-body, either with "floating" pickups added, or with pickups built-in. Gibson was still considered the leading brand for jazz guitarists, and many players chose from the company's best electric-acoustic models, the Super 400CES and the L-5CES. Both had been launched in the early 1950s, but during 1960 a design change occurred when the earlier "rounded" cutaway style was changed to a "sharp" cutaway, providing improved high-fret access. Wes Montgomery, the most famous jazz guitarist of the 1960s, often used a custom L-5CES with one pickup.

WES MONTGOMERY made 19 albums for Riverside, including this 1961 record (left), until the label closed in 1964 and the guitarist shifted to Verve. Around 1962 he told writer Ralph Gleason that he'd tried conventional plectrum picking for a few months but came back to his unusual thumb-picking style, opting for feel over precision. "I just didn't like the sound [of the plectrum]," said Montgomery, "I liked the tone better with the thumb, but the technique better with the pick. But I couldn't have them both."

Shadows, and it became a UK number one hit in January 1963. Page would go on to perform on countless British pop hits throughout the 1960s with artists as diverse as Val Doonican, Them, Lulu, Herman's Hermits and Joe Cocker, among many others. Page had also produced Eric Clapton's first recordings with John Mayall back in 1965. As a consequence of this wide exposure to so many different styles, Page had become something of a musical magpie, stealing or borrowing from a broad range of influences yet never really excelling in any one particular field.

In the summer of 1966 Page had been persuaded to join The Yardbirds. Initially he was the bass player, but within a couple of months he'd moved back to guitar to form a potentially world-beating partnership with Jeff Beck. It didn't last long. Beck quit the group that November, leaving Page to keep the band afloat until its eventual demise in the summer of 1968. As The Yardbirds were still under contract to undertake a Scandinavian tour in August, Page had to find musicians to form a new line-up of the band. On bass he enlisted his old friend from the studio years, John Paul Jones, plus two relative unknowns from central England, drummer John Bonham and vocalist Robert Plant. Before the end of the year they'd dropped The New Yardbirds name and retreated to the studio to record their first LP.

Few could have predicted the impact that the record would make on its release in March 1969. Page drew on the vast experience he'd gained in his studio years, creating some awe-inspiring sounds from an eclectic variety of sources: Eddie Phillips' violin-bow technique played through wah-wah; huge reverb-drenched acoustic guitars; heavily distorted slide guitar à la Jeff Beck (whose recent solo album *Truth* had clearly been a huge influence); pedal-steel guitar, hitherto unheard of outside country circles; and some truly exciting guitar solos, electronically double-tracked to stunning effect. Page had even borrowed from Bert Jansch, whose 1966 interpretation of 'Blackwater Side' he'd again updated (Page had previously adapted it as 'White Summer' for The Yardbirds). Page added a tabla player for the Zeppelin interpretation and rechristened it 'Black Mountain Side'. No longer a folk tune, it had become in his hands an acoustic rock performance, made possible by Page's abundant skill and knowledge of the recording studio.

LED ZEP II: whole lotta riffs.

The foundation for the kaleidoscope of musical colours evident on the first Zeppelin album was the super-solid rhythm section of Jones and Bonham, giving much weight to Plant's unearthly vocal delivery. The whole record throbbed with a dark, eerie power which would set a course for the heavy rock/metal phenomenon that would follow into the 1970s. In October, a second album would be released, even heavier and more dynamic than the first, with Page again in the producer's chair, deploying the studio almost as another instrument as he used and abused all its facilities in his quest for bigger and heavier sounds.

Pop musicians were by now gaining a strong sense of self importance, as record sales increased with the rise of the new youth culture, bringing wealth and adulation to the lucky successful ones. Groups and singers were no longer 'pop stars', but preferred to be thought of as Artists. This pretentious attitude would be reflected in the music that attracted the term 'progressive rock'. True, the music scene was a far more interesting place than it had been ten years earlier; now, hundreds of talented, intelligent musicians were following the examples set by The Beatles and Bob Dylan. These highly motivated people applied much serious thought and diligence to their pursuit of a higher craft.

The Who, former west London R&B terrorists turned pop art hit-makers, released in May 1969 their 90-minute 'rock opera'

Tommy, an early example of an unfortunate trend toward 'concept albums' that would become prevalent in the 1970s. New acts like Yes and Jethro Tull made their mark over the summer releasing albums packed with original and inventive songs that overstepped the four-minute barrier, oblivious to the fact that they were unlikely to be heard in the singles charts. In the US, Frank Zappa, a serious composer and social commentator whose instrument of choice was the electric guitar, broke through with a successful album of pieces highlighting his compositional skills and solo improvisations. There were certainly no hit singles on *Hot Rats*.

It was also the year of the summer rock festival, culminating in the massive Woodstock Music & Art Fair held in upstate New York in August 1969. The Woodstock festival seemed to serve as an international celebration of everything the 1960s had achieved in popular music, and in the new culture of the young. Folkies rubbed shoulders with blues bands, soul icons mingled effortlessly with psychedelic blissniks, and all were gathered together under the corporate umbrella labelled 'rock'.

HOT RATS, hot guitars, 1969.

Latin-American music established its place in the mélange through a new group from America's West Coast named for its leader and guitarist Carlos Santana. By fusing the sound of a loud, blues guitar with the exciting native percussion of South America, yet another ethnic tradition was welcomed to the fold. Elsewhere, jazz would soon follow; British guitarist John McLaughlin had relocated to the US to work with Miles Davis and with drummer Tony Williams, grunging up his sound in the process and paving the way for what would eventually mutate into jazz-rock fusion in the coming decade.

In November 1969 a curious double-album appeared from Captain Beefheart & His Magic Band, *Trout Mask Replica*. Produced by Frank Zappa, the record contained some of the most unorthodox guitar playing yet heard. It featured the unusual talents of guitarists Zoot Horn Rollo and Winged Eel Fingerling, their bizarre style having developed as a result of being forced to duplicate note-perfect the somewhat eccentric piano playing style of the good Captain. Uniquely original, The Magic Band would remain strangers to commercial success, yet their influence in guitar playing circles is still evident in many modern styles.

Possibly the most ambitious album of 1969 came from a new group from the west of England, King Crimson. Led by the group's guitar-scientist Robert Fripp, *In The Court Of The Crimson King* was so far ahead of its time that it would represent for years the high water mark of the progressive era. The record's standout track was the sinister '21st Century Schizoid Man', a seven-and-a-half-minute epic in three movements. A heavy rock riff accelerates into a series of avant-garde guitar and Mellotron solos over a jazzy 6/8 bass and drums accompaniment, and then breaks down into a ludicrous stop-start guitar-and-drum duet that had players and musicologists scratching their heads in disbelief.

Fripp's guitar technique incorporated a deadly accurate right-hand picking style, developed in part from hours spent as a youth attempting to play The Spotnicks' 1962 British hit 'Orange Blossom Special' up to speed... unaware of the varispeed tape trickery involved in its recording. But light-years had passed since then; whatever influences had soaked into his consciousness in the interim, they were far from obvious. Robert Fripp was an original, as he remains to this day. Perhaps '21st Century Schizoid Man' best illustrates, more than mere words, just how far popular music had travelled in this most turbulent of decades, while also acting as an ominous pointer to the direction it would take in the 1970s. ■ DAVE GREGORY

FRIPP's guitar science course.

HARMONY claimed to be the world's biggest guitar-maker of the 1960s. Models such as the H-75 shown on this 1960 catalogue (left) served to introduce the electric guitar to many a young player. One such was Keith Richards (far left) who used a Harmony Meteor in the early days of his musical career with The Rolling Stones.

△ HARMONY METEOR H-70
Produced 1960-1968; this example c1965

Harmony, based in Chicago, did a good job turning out plenty of mid-priced, average guitars for aspiring guitarists of the 1960s, providing players such as Keith Richards – seen playing his Meteor above – with a cheap instrument to get things rolling. Left-handed versions such as this are rarely encountered.

ELVIS PRESLEY leaves the army for a film career. Eddie Cochran is killed in a car crash on his way to London Airport.

A NEW £1 banknote design is issued in Britain, the first to show Queen Elizabeth. The farthing coin, worth just a quarter of a penny, is withdrawn from circulation.

FIFTY-SIX black South Africans are killed by police in Sharpeville, Transvaal. Later, prime minister Verwoerd is shot in an assassination attempt.

ALFRED HITCHCOCK deploys a TV crew and a tiny budget to set the movie Psycho in a lonely motel owned by psychopathic Norman Bates. The shower room is shared.

Gibson, the workingman's guitar.

Wes Montgomery & Gibson at work for MGM/Verve records.

scoring, it captures Montgomery's reflective side perfectly and showcases his ability to breathe life into a melody with sensitive single-line and chordal statements.

When Riverside ceased recording activities in 1964, the guitarist switched to the Verve label, and producer Creed Taylor pushed Montgomery more and more into a commercial direction. Some exciting jazz albums emerged from this association in its early days, but following the success of *Goin' Out Of My Head*, which won a Grammy award in 1967 for Best Instrumental Jazz Performance, Taylor increasingly restricted Montgomery's creative role on the records. Gone were the extended solos which had allowed the guitarist to unfold and develop ideas; now he rarely got more than a chorus of improvisation on each piece, while the trademark 'octaves' sound was brought to the fore and emphasised almost to the point of cliché. Montgomery was swathed in strings, struggling to extract musical value from trivial material. On the plus side, the records did get valuable radio airing and sold in quantities of which most jazz producers could only dream.

Sadly, Montgomery had only a short time to enjoy this success. He died of a heart attack on June 15th 1968 at age 43. The impact of this artist on the development of the guitar in jazz cannot be overstated. For many jazz players and listeners it was Montgomery who finally brought the guitar from the periphery to centre-stage as a jazz instrument. He was steeped in the language of jazz – a jazz musician first and a guitarist second. He'd absorbed the current innovations and could play the jazz music of the period with the authority of a star saxophonist and, like all great jazz artists, he was equally

AN AMERICAN U2 spy plane is shot down over Russia in May. The flight is described as a "weather research" mission, but the Russians sentence pilot Gary Powers to ten years' detention. He is released in February of the following year, exchanged for a Soviet spy.

LADY Chatterley's Lover, D.H. Lawrence's 1920s novel about the sexual exploits of Chatterley and her gamekeeper, is found not obscene by a London court. The judge famously asked the jury, "Is it a book you would wish your wife or servant to read?" After the trial 200,000 copies are sold immediately.

1961

GEORGE BENSON began recording in his own right in the 1960s with records like this 1966 LP, although his greatest success came in the following decade with luxurious pop-jazz records such as Breezin'. An assured technician with a penchant for hard, driving bop and an ear for melody, Benson had started playing sessions as a teenager with organists Jimmy Smith and Brother Jack McDuff. But once he'd been spotted by Wes Montgomery a record contract was inevitable, and he signed to Columbia. In the 1960s Benson most often used the Gibson Super 400 (pictured on the album sleeve, right), as well as picking on a D'Angelico and a Guild.

strong on ballads and up-tempo numbers and could play a soulful blues. Montgomery had extended the vocabulary of the strong on ballads and up-tempo numbers and could play a soulful blues. Montgomery had extended the vocabulary of the guitar in jazz and his octaves and block-chord runs had introduced a new sound to the music.

There can be few jazz guitarists since 1960 who owe nothing to the influence of Wes Montgomery. Among the many who freely admit to Montgomery as an inspiration are Larry Coryell, Lee Ritenour, Pat Metheny, George Benson, the late Emily Remler, Terry Smith, Jim Mullen, Ronnie Jordan and, not least, Pat Martino.

During the 1960s Martino had become friendly with Montgomery and frequently jammed and worked on musical ideas with him. A professional musician from age 15, Martino had a robust, round sound, and under the influence of plectrum-guitar master Johnny Smith developed a formidable technique. The legacy of the association with Montgomery is most evident in Martino's fluent octave passages which were such a hallmark of Wes's style. But it was Martino's brilliance as an improviser – his ability to weave long, involved melodic lines through any chord progression with unerring drive and swing – that gave him his own identity. And on albums such as 1967's El Hombre Martino underlined his confident approach and solid jazz chops, but also applied a questing spirit to research possibilities beyond mainstream jazz, demonstrating his interest in typical late-1960s passions such as Indian music and jazz-rock fusion. A contrast to Montgomery and Martino was Joe Pass, the epitome of the all-round jazz guitarist. A superb single-line improviser with an impeccable technique, Pass was also an outstanding accompanist and chordal player. His mastery of bebop harmony and his ability to apply it to the guitar were legendary, but his technical skill was counterbalanced by an equally profound artistic sense, so that the results were always truly musical. Born in 1929 and raised in the Italian community of Philadelphia, Pass's promising career was interrupted by a 12-year period of drug dependence, and he finally entered the Synanon drug rehabilitation clinic in 1960 at the age of 31, staying for three years. A recording he made there in 1961 with fellow patients, Sounds Of Synanon, signalled his talent to the wider public and, after leaving the clinic, two outstanding albums, Catch Me and For Django, firmly established his reputation as a brilliant and soulful improviser whose clear, melodic lines sounded fresh and relaxed at any tempo. From the early 1970s Pass would develop an innovative unaccompanied style, epitomised by Virtuoso.

The 1960s were exciting years for popular music. The

△ GIBSON BARNEY KESSEL CUSTOM
Produced 1961-1971; this example March 1967

Gibson produced a number of new "signature" models in the 1960s named for jazz players such as Barney Kessel, who had been the most famous jazz guitarist of the 1950s. The body of his Gibson featured an unusual twin "sharp" cutaway.

THE BRILLIANT improviser Pat Martino made his finest album, El Hombre (far left), in 1967. Joe Pass came back from drug dependence to record the outstanding Catch Me LP (centre) in 1962, while at the very end of the decade John McLaughlin's first solo album appeared, the adventurous Extrapolation (left).

BARNEY KESSEL (below) wears a bow-tie in this Gibson promo shot to echo the "bow-tie" fingerboard markers of the Barney Kessel model.

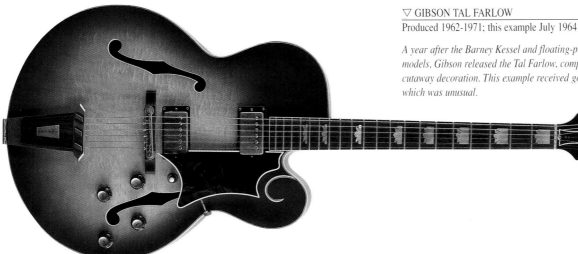

worldwide dissemination of blues music, the explosion of talent in rock music and the emergence of the new breed of singer-songwriters changed the face of the music industry forever. But while many profited, others lost. For many established jazz musicians the release of the first Beatles, Stones and Dylan albums coincided with the end of their careers. As the public's attention shifted from jazz to rock, so the jazz clubs closed or changed their music policy, and sales of jazz records declined.

But the younger generation of jazz guitarists coming up in the 1960s could hardly ignore the blues and rock music that surrounded them. Indeed many, like John McLaughlin and Larry Coryell, had progressed to jazz from an initial interest in blues or rock. In the midst of this revolution, London's jazz scene in the mid-1960s was a hotbed of musical experimentation and development. While some musicians were rejecting the established structures of post-bebop jazz in favour of a freer approach to improvisation, others were blending elements of blues and rock with jazz.

John McLaughlin arrived in London from the north-east of England and immersed himself in this activity, working in a music store by day and playing in groups by night alongside Alexis Korner, Georgie Fame, Graham Bond, Jack Bruce and trumpeters Ian Carr and Kenny Wheeler. McLaughlin's driving guitar style had more than an echo of saxophonist John Coltrane's contemporary jazz approach, but also reflected his early interest in the blues of Muddy Waters and the jazz guitar of Django Reinhardt and Tal Farlow. By the late 1960s

McLaughlin too had begun to study Indian music, and recorded his first album as a leader, *Extrapolation*.

Moving to New York in 1969, McLaughlin recorded with Miles Davis, and *In A Silent Way* signalled the beginning of jazz-rock fusion. But it was McLaughlin's work with drummer Tony Williams' group Lifetime that finally confirmed him as an innovative guitarist of immense talent. Lifetime performed with extraordinary intensity and its complex rhythms, demanding tempos, intricate melodies and dissonant harmonies outlined a fresh musical language. No other jazz or rock guitarist could approach McLaughlin for rhythmic and harmonic sense, or inventive power. Later McLaughlin would form the Mahavishnu Orchestra which came to define guitar-led fusion in the 1970s.

The influence of outstanding players active outside jazz in the 1960s such as B.B. King and Jimi Hendrix transcended stylistic boundaries and filtered into jazz guitar in many ways. Players opted for solidbody guitars alongside the traditional archtop Gibsons and fitted lighter-gauge strings for greater string-bending facility. Improvising over a rock pulse as readily as jazz swing, they sought inspiration in the simpler chords of rock music and the cyclic harmonies of bebop.

By the end of the 1960s many jazz guitarists were no longer content simply to replicate the music of the saxophone and other jazz instruments on the guitar. They were prepared to use the unique sounds and qualities of the electric guitar to create a fresh vocabulary and assume a leading role in the jazz-rock fusion of the 1970s. ■ **CHARLES ALEXANDER**

YURI GAGARIN is the first man in space. The Russian orbits earth in Vostok-1 for a little under two hours. A month later Alan Shepherd is the first American in space, fired 116 miles up for a 15-minute leap. In August, Gherman Titov orbits in Vostok-2 for 25 hours.

GEORGE FORMBY, British screen star and ukulele wizard, dies. David Evans is born in Dublin, Ireland; at the end of the next decade he will become guitarist Edge in U2.

THE BERLIN WALL is built to prevent East Berliners reaching the West. Elsewhere the contraceptive pill goes on general sale, aimed to control more personal incursions.

CATCH-22, Joseph Heller's comic-surreal novel about American airmen in the wartime Mediterranean, is published. The title will pass into the language to describe deadlock.

THE TWIST is the latest dance craze to rock America. Less rhythmically bound, Bob Dylan debuts in New York folk clubs and is signed to the Columbia record company in September.

▽ GIBSON TAL FARLOW

Produced 1962-1971; this example July 1964

A year after the Barney Kessel and floating-pickup Johnny Smith models, Gibson released the Tal Farlow, complete with its ornate cutaway decoration. This example received gold-plated hardware, which was unusual.

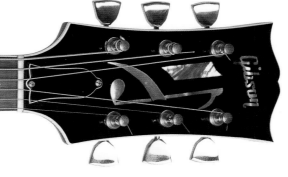

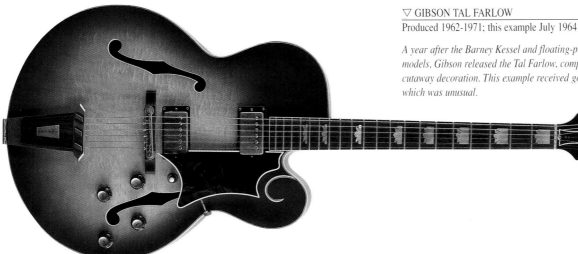

AMERICA's recently elected president John F Kennedy faces trouble abroad as an invasion of Cuba at the Bay of Pigs fails, and as the number of "military advisers" sent by the US to Vietnam steadily increases.

RICKENBACKER made one of the first electric guitars back in the 1930s, and during the 1960s established themselves through the use of their stylish, modern guitars by The Beatles and The Byrds. Later in the decade, the company's 1968 catalogue cover (left) reflected the fashionable op-art style of the time, mirroring the work of artists such as Bridget Riley.

▽ RICKENBACKER 460
Produced 1961-1985; this example 1961

An idiosyncratic maker based in California, Rickenbacker introduced two of its most distinctive features on the 460: a control layout with an extra fifth "blend" knob, and triangle fingerboard markers.

▽ GRETSCH CHET ATKINS COUNTRY GENTLEMAN
Produced 1961-1981 (this style); this example 1963

Chet Atkins had helped design a number of Gretsch models since the mid 1950s. The thin-bodied Country Gentleman, for example, had first appeared in 1957, but during 1961 Gretsch launched an updated version with a twin-cutaway body for better high-fret access. It became enormously popular after George Harrison, a big Atkins fan, took up the guitar in 1963 and used it on many of The Beatles' live dates.

COLLECTOR'S ITEM!

Ready for the Storms?

THE IN SOUND IS ENGLISH

ELECTRIC GUITARS became so popular in the 1960s that even flat-top guitar makers such as Ovation (centre) and Martin (far left) tried to sell electrics. Guitar distributors sought out electric suppliers and invented new brands – St Louis Music created Custom Kraft (left), for example – while old hands like Kay (inset, below centre) just upped production and enjoyed the cash-flow.

AMERICAN GUITARS

The two most revered US guitar makers of the 1960s, Gibson and Fender, are covered elsewhere in this book. But what of the other American companies whose instruments fuelled the decade's music? How did they deal with the boom in electric guitars following The Beatles' arrival on US soil in 1964, and did they survive the slump at the end of the 1960s? Here we consider ten years' output from the likes of Rickenbacker, Gretsch and Harmony, to National, Danelectro and Mosrite.

Throughout most of the 1960s an old guitar was called 'used', not 'vintage', and players didn't think about its value unless they were trading it in for something flashier. People looked ahead to a thrilling future, not back to a romanticised past. I mean, a double-cutaway must be better than a single-cut. Why? Because it's new, it's different... and Gretsch says so. What more do you need to know?

In the previous decade, departures from tradition had been the exceptions. Dealers maligned Flying Vs because they weren't, well, Gibson-like. But some of those departures became the new norms, and by the 1960s the defining philosophy dictated that innovation wasn't a bonus – it was expected. The go-go vibe was described by Andrew Edelstein in *The Pop Sixties* as "the spirit of the now" and it permeated everything from paisley pullovers to presidential politics.

For guitar buyers it was a time of unprecedented variety. Small firms like Carvin continued to build reliable solidbodies, while Micro-Frets offered wireless guitars with built-in FM transmitters and length-adjustable string nuts. Archtop master builder Jimmy D'Aquisto brought the highest standards of craftsmanship to electric designs. Even the historic Martin company dipped its toes into the electric stream with their DeArmond-pickup-equipped F-series archtops.

Of course, by the dawn of the 1960s the pillars of the electric temple were already in place: Les Pauls, Strats, Teles, classic Rickenbackers and Gretsches. In fact, most of them had preceded the rock'n'roll for which they would prove so suitable. But if in the 1950s the gear had led the music, in the 1960s it was often the other way around. The unrelenting demand for guitars left manufacturers struggling to catch up, to look cool, even to survive. In retrospect some of their 1960s 'innovations' look more like mere refinements, and some were borderline silly. Still, there were important advances among the rush.

A turning point occurred on February 8th 1964 when George Harrison encountered his first Rickenbacker electric 12-string. He was quite taken with it and debuted it on the cowbell-bonkin' intro to 'You Can't Do That'. Sitting in a Hollywood theatre, Jim (later Roger) McGuinn saw *A Hard Day's Night* and he, too, fell in love with the keening chime of the 12-string Rick; thus was born the instrumental sound of The Byrds (it's not much fun to imagine 'Mr. Tambourine Man' performed on an SG). Many of the decade's finest records – The Beatles' 'A Hard Day's Night',

The Byrds' 'Eight Miles High', The Who's 'I Can't Explain' – were energised by the jingle-jangle of the Rick 12, one of the decade's greatest contributions to guitar design.

In fact, Rickenbacker popularised a slew of advances during the 1960s, including Rick-O-Sound stereo and a brilliantly engineered headstock that allowed 12 tuners to fit on a standard sized peghead, avoiding the top-heaviness of most 12-string guitars. Other ideas never got off the ground, such as slanted frets, or the Convertible guitars that featured interesting if unwieldy comb-and-handle contraptions intended to pull six strings out of the way, converting a 12-string to a regular guitar.

At Gretsch, the seeds of innovation and whimsy planted in the 1950s came to full flower in the 1960s, with feature-laden heavy cruisers like the Viking and the White Falcon, typically with Super'Tron or 12-screw patent-number Filter'Tron pickups. The big news was the shift to double cutaways for the leading models in '61 and '62, but otherwise there was little in the line that had not been introduced or at least foreshadowed in the previous decade. Exceptions included the Monkees six-string; a vaguely 335-ish 12-string; and the seldom-seen Bikini, a double-neck with slide-in, fold-up components reminiscent of some automatic weapons.

While these guitars may not rival their single-cut forebears as top-rung collectibles, they're among the Gretschiest Gretsches ever, some sporting a mix of 1950s carryovers and 1960s ideas like angled frets, sealed hollow bodies (with fake f-holes), twin 'mufflers' (string mutes), Tone Twister vibratos, telescoping whammy handles, interior tuning forks, 'zero' frets, whoopie

GRETSCH enjoyed a huge increase in business during the 1960s, and struggled to survive the cramped New York factory they had occupied since 1916. So in 1965 Gretsch's drum operation was moved to another site and the guitar workspace expanded, as these shots (right) inside the Brooklyn HQ reveal.

CHET ATKINS (right) was country music's best known guitar-picker of the 1960s, and gave Gretsch priceless publicity for their Chet Atkins models.

INSTRUMENT makers rushed into the booming 1960s guitar market. Even Wurlitzer, best *known for mighty organs, joined in (below) as this 1966 ad for the Wildcat announces.*

cushions (oops, I mean back pads), and even more switches and knobs than their predecessors. The Chet Atkins Hollow Body (or Nashville) was one of the decade's most lusted-after guitars; the double-cut Country Gent remains a classic by any standard; and for sheer brazenness, will any major-name guitar ever surpass or even approach the gadget-encrusted mid-1960s stereo White Falcon, the apotheosis of unabashed gizmomania?

During World War II, National-Dobro was reorganised as Valco. After the war, it bought bodies and parts from Rickenbacker, Kay, Harmony, Regal and others, part of a trend which helped lend a mix-and-match quality to so many moderately priced instruments (Valco built guitars under the Silvertone, Airline, and Oahu brands; some of its own guitars even had Gibson bodies). Although the Valco company still used the National brand in the 1960s, it generally abandoned the resonator guitars that had brought it to prominence, concentrating instead on electrics with unique shapes, colourful finishes, fragile whammies and silkscreened pickup covers. While Valco is fondly remembered for its budget models, its best guitars weren't cheap. A Glenwood 99, for example, cost as much as Gibson's gold-plated, triple-humbucker SG Custom.

Valco exec Al Frost told me, "We started using plastic more

and more... we'd take plastic, which was just like a rubber glove, and cement it to the guitars and trim it off. With the electrics you didn't need all that resonance, so we tried making the bodies out of polyester resin and fibreglass. We would take a mould, spray the finish in, then the fibreglass, pull it out of there, and the finish would already be on it. Oh, it was beautiful," Frost concluded.

This embrace of plastics technology along with an exploration of the mid-priced market niche meshed nicely with the industrial approach that had characterised National-Dobro from the beginning. By the early 1960s Valco was offering a wide selection of National and generally cheaper Supro electrics, some conventional in appearance and others like nothing players had ever seen. This latter category included Res-O-Glas models, blending fibreglass bodies with standard necks and hardware. If you wanted to step up from your bargain-basement Harmony and couldn't afford an Epiphone – or you just liked the idea of a turquoise guitar shaped like a map of the United States – then Valco was the place to go.

Valco wouldn't survive long past the mid-decade commercial tidal wave. It became involved with Kay in a complicated financial tangle and, as Al Frost put it, "When Kay sank, Valco sank." But its last-gasp guitars included nifty

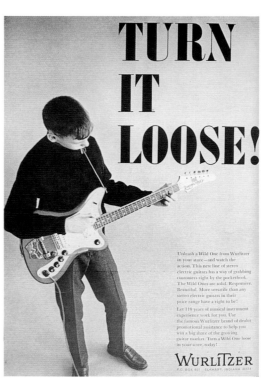

EPIPHONE was established in the early 20th century, soon enjoying a reputation for top-quality archtop guitars. But by the 1950s Epi was in disarray, and Gibson bought the ailing operation in 1957. A revitalised line was introduced amid more go-ahead publicity, such as this striking 1964 catalogue (left).

AL CAIOLA (left) was a respected studio session guitarist who helped Epiphone design his 1963 "signature" guitar. It borrowed the five-way "Tonexpressor" tone circuit that the company had introduced a year earlier on its Professional model. Neither guitar proved very popular.

▽ EPIPHONE SHERATON E212T
Produced 1961-1970 (this style); this example November 1961

At first Epiphone prospered under its new owner, Gibson, which developed Epi as a separate but related line. Unfortunately, this led some people to view Epiphone as a kind of second-rate Gibson – although as fine guitars such as this Sheraton prove, this was far from the truth. Nonetheless, Epi sales declined, and in 1970 the brand was moved to Japanese-made guitars.

TED McCARTY (left), Gibson's president until 1966 when he left for Bigsby, controlled the Epiphone lines with production manager Ward Arbanas. Epis were built alongside Gibsons at the Kalamazoo factory.

CALIFORNIA not only hosted well known guitar makers such as Rickenbacker and Mosrite during the 1960s, but also saw the blossoming of many smaller operations. One such outfit was Magnatone, whose 1965 catalogue (left) was inhabated by clean-cut West-coasters just short of plausible grooviness.

HARMONY's Rocket model (above) was an unmistakable 1960s guitar, with its impressive curve of control knobs skirting the lower half of the body. Although they had a simple application – a volume and tone control for each of the guitar's three pickups – the multiple controls hinted that only a rocket scientist could be trusted with such a handful.

models like the $99.50 Belmont; the Bermuda, with an onboard electronic tremolo and "brilliant polyester cherry" finish; and the company's highly collectable map-shape Glenwoods, Val-Pros, Newports and Westwoods.

By the time it folded in 1968, Danelectro had become dear to the hearts of players everywhere. Most Dan'os of the 1960s were updates of late-1950s models, including hollow guitars shaped like solidbodies, and pseudo-solidbodies with pine frames, Masonite (hardboard) tops and backs, pebbled-vinyl side coverings, and those inimitable lipstick-tube pickups (which sounded great, by the way). Danelectro sold truckloads of guitars to mail-order company Sears, who distributed them under the Silvertone brand along with models made by Harmony and others.

Founder Nat Daniel's biggest contribution was a production savvy that allowed him to put cool, low-priced guitars into the hands of countless players – his stack-pot double-neck retailed for $175 – but his New Jersey-based company introduced significant new ideas, too, like the amp-in-the-case set. One period piece was an electric sitar marketed under the Coral name; complete with body-mounted drone strings and a buzzy 'Sitarmatic' bridge, it added what passed for a Middle Eastern tinge to several hits. Another Coral took the unusual course of combining Danelectro's lyre-shaped 'Longhorn' silhouette with

△ GIBSON SG/LES PAUL STANDARD
Produced 1961-1963; this example November 1961

This was one of Gibson's new-in-1961 guitars, known now as SG/Les Paul models because they had the new SG body shape but (at least at first) kept the "Les Paul" name on the instrument.

COLLECTORS value the limited number of Customs that have this vibrato bridge (left) with an attractive inlaid ebony block adjoining the tailpiece.

a hollow body to produce one of the oddest guitars of the decade. Then there were Mosrites, the brainchildren of the late Semie Moseley, an amiable gospel musician from Bakersfield, California, who had worked for Rickenbacker. The soft-spoken Oklahoma transplant built an eye-poppin' double-neck for superpicker Joe Maphis, but it was a mid-1960s association with The Ventures that put his instruments on the map. Among the most distinctive guitars of the era, they featured curvy sculpted bodies, beautiful finishes, and ultra-low actions nicely complemented by feather-touch Vibramute tailpieces. Back in 1980, Moseley told me with a laugh, "All I did was to take a Fender, flop it over and trace around it .... [the shape] was just an upside-down Fender." The mainstays of Mosrite were the successful Ventures models, but the line was rounded out with a variety of other models that included 12-strings, basses and hollowbody guitars.

Guild's Duane Eddy models were a bit odd in one respect: Eddy had recorded his twangy landmark hits on a DeArmond-equipped Gretsch 6120, not a Guild. At any rate, Guild's Duane Eddy archtops were beautiful instruments. Two of Guild's most unusual designs were associated with jazz titan

George Barnes: the AcoustiLectric, and the small-bodied Guitar In F. Neither had soundholes, and on both the pickups were suspended in holes in the top to minimise interference with top vibration. Among the most collectible of all the 1960s Guild guitars are the hollow-body versions that the company made of the BluesBird, variations on the compact, single-cutaway Aristocrat, which Guild described as a "light-weight, semisolid midget model".

Guild's thin-body Starfires were well-made guitars somewhat reminiscent of Gibson thinlines; they came in both single- and double-cutaway versions, usually in cherry red. Guild also excelled in building jazz-style archtops, such as the Epiphone-inspired Stratford; it was equipped with six tone pushbuttons that looked a little clunky but were more versatile than any stock Strat or Les Paul Custom. One of the more unusual features introduced by Guild during the 1960s that didn't catch on among other makers was the hinged guitar stand set into the backs of Thunderbirds and Polaras.

By mid-decade Kay had moved into a huge new facility near Chicago's O'Hare airport and was producing up to a reported 1,500 guitars a day, most of them budget models that allowed countless aspiring rockers to get started on electric guitar.

Kay's Jazz II, for example, one of many double-cutaways more or less derived from Gibson's 335, featured big pickups with grid-pattern covers and a V-crested peghead that owed more to rocket-inspired auto styling (or perhaps modernistic coffee-shop appliances) than any guitar tradition. The guitar boom tapered off rapidly, leaving Kay hopelessly over-extended. By the end of the decade it had changed hands several times, but none of the new owners could save it, and in 1969 the Kay brandname was ignominiously sold at auction.

Kay's history was paralleled by Harmony's. Both were old Midwestern companies that moved into enlarged facilities just in time for the mid-1960s surge and then faltered as the boom subsided and imports increased. Harmony president Chuck Rubovits told me that in the 1964-65 production cycle Harmony employed 600 workers, produced more than 1000 guitars a day, and grossed $11 million. By 1968, he estimated, Harmony was making most of the guitars produced in America, certainly more than anyone else. Before the company fell to the same market forces that had toppled Kay, it produced a vast amount of reasonably good-quality budget electrics (some of them sold through the Sears mail-order operation). A typical example of a 1960s Harmony was the

SOLID HIT
the Les Paul guitars
by GIBSON

Les Paul and Mary Ford: two solid hits on the list of all-time guitar greats. With their own brand of sound, big and bright...with special styling and effects—they reach enhance through every medium. Whether it's radio, night club, TV, a Columbia recording, or a dinner engagement...Les and Mary are always a solid hit—and it's always with their Gibson guitars.

Just out—did a solid session with guitar players—saw the new Les Paul Model solid body Gibsons. Ultra thin, hand contoured, double cutaway...with new Gibson Vibrato and the famous "fretless wonder" neck (a low, fast action neck giving the ultimate in playing ease and rapidity).

This dynamic Les Paul series is an exciting new approach to the solid body guitar. Beauty in gleaming white or cherry red that must be seen. Wonderfully close feel-like tone that must be heard. Fast action that should be tried....now. By Gibson, of course.

Gibson
KALAMAZOO, MICHIGAN

LES PAUL and Mary Ford (left), the husband-and-wife duo who had enjoyed big hits in the 1950s, fell from favour in the 1960s, and divorced in 1963. Paul did not renew his contract with Gibson, fearful of new earnings being sucked into divorce settlements, and so the SG guitars stopped appearing with "Les Paul" on them.

△ GIBSON SG SPECIAL
Produced 1961-1971 (this style); this example
January 1966

The SG-body version of the Special never appeared with the Les Paul name on the instrument. This SG Special was originally finished in Pelham Blue, but the top coat of clear lacquer has yellowed with age to make it look green.

LES PAUL (below right) first shot to fame in the early 1950s with hit records such as 'How High The Moon' which bristled with plentiful layered-up guitars in brilliant homemade productions. Les Paul & Mary Ford continued to record into the early 1960s, but by 1963 the duo was personally as well as professionally finished. However, Paul emerged from his "retirement" in 1968 with the Les Paul Now! LP, re-recordings of his best material, and the same year Gibson bowed to popular demand and reissued the original-design Les Paul models (see also p.70).

△ GIBSON SG/LES PAUL CUSTOM
Produced 1961-1963; this example October 1962

Because of declining sales and a feeling that their solidbody guitars were beginning to look old fashioned, Gibson completely redesigned the Les Paul Junior, Standard and Custom models in 1961 with this modern twin-cutaway body. The "Les Paul" name was dropped during 1963, and Gibson began to call the new models the SG Junior, SG Standard and SG Custom.

three-pickup Rocket III, with a hard-to-miss crescent of six big white knobs along the lower bout.

While the joint was jumpin' at established companies, some of the boldest ideas were coming from newcomers like Dan Armstrong, a New York repairman/designer who at the end of the decade came up with one of the era's most intriguing guitars. For the body he chose a hard, clear plastic, but not for the easy-production reasons behind Valco's Res-O-Glas models. Armstrong said, "My intention was to make a guitar that sustained extremely well," thus invoking a consideration that dominated design discussions for years.

Although best remembered for their see-through bodies, Armstrong's Ampeg-made guitars also featured inter-changeable, slide-in pickups co-designed by Bill Lawrence. The idea that a player could readily change pickups for different applications helped spawn a near-obsession with versatility that would characterise scads of multi-switch/coil-tap designs in the coming decade. But the biggest contribution of Dan Armstrong and other like-minded builders of the 1960s was more subtle than any single feature. It was, simply, the notion that the industry giants hadn't taken the electric guitar as far as it could go after all. ■ TOM WHEELER

KAY had by 1961 become one of the biggest guitar producers in America, as this expansive view (above) of its new Chicago factory in 1964 conspicuously demonstrates. The company dates back to 1890, although the brandname itself was not used until the 1930s. A group of investors bought Kay in 1955

and ex-Harmony man Sidney Katz became president. He turned Kay into another Harmony by aiming primarily at mass sales of budget guitars. By 1964 Kay had made its 2,000,000th guitar. During the flurry of corporate buy-outs of guitar makers in 1965, Seeburg, a vending machine

company, bought Kay. In 1966 Katz resigned amid losses and "mutual disappointment". Meanwhile Valco, owner of the National brand, bought Kay from Seeburg in 1967, but Kay took Valco with it when it folded in 1969. Both the Kay and National brandnames were sold at auction that year.

THE SHADOWS became the biggest endorsers of Burns guitars when Hank Marvin spurned his famous Strat and helped to design the 1964 Burns Marvin model (seen, right, with Marvin, centre, and Bruce Welch, far right). Other Burns guitars included the Split Sonic and Vista Sonic models, as displayed in this shot from the 1963 catalogue (left).

△ BURNS BISON
Produced 1961-1962 (this style); this example 1961

Britain's supreme moment of 1960s guitar engineering, the Bison was a handbuilt four-pickup wonder that was the aim of every flagwaving beat-group musician. But at £157 it was pure unattainable luxury for most, on the same level as an imported Strat (£148), and at a time when the average knockabout electric could be had for around £20. According to one insider, only 49 four-pickup Bisons were made before a "simplified" three-pickup version replaced it during 1962. The four-pickup Bison is one of the finest (and rarest) British guitars ever made.

EUROPEAN GUITARS

An embargo on US musical instrument imports to the UK was lifted during the summer of 1959, and the following year American-made guitars at last began to hit British shores. Players thought they'd never had it so good. Long-desired but hitherto unobtainable transatlantic electrics came over in quantity, and at first it seemed as if guitars made closer to home were in danger of being forgotten in the rush. Sales of un-American instruments did suffer, of course, but soon a new picture emerged.

In 1960s Britain, as now, the leading players exerted a great influence on those striving to emulate their styles and successes. Guitars fingered by the famous were important. While local hero Bert Weedon stolidly stuck with his Höfners, rising guitar star Hank B. Marvin had other ideas. He was assuming an increasingly high profile as lead guitarist in Cliff Richard's backing band, The Shadows, and inspiring a multitude of imitators. Marvin's Buddy Holly-like horn-rimmed glasses may have made a big impression, but it was his red Fender Stratocaster that became the main focus of attention for a multitude of aspiring axe-wielders.

That Fiesta Red Strat had come direct from America in the

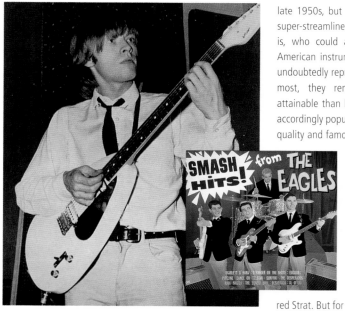

VOX guitars, originally made by Jennings in Dartford, Kent, were seen with the famous (Brian Jones with distinctive

two-pickup teardrop Mk VI, above) and the not-so-famous (the "other" Eagles, right, with a handful of Vox Fendalikes).

late 1950s, but now anyone could go and buy one of these super-streamlined solids in their local music shop. Anyone, that is, who could afford it. To many hopeful British players, American instruments were over here and overpriced. While undoubtedly representing the epitome of design and sound to most, they remained mere dream machines, no more attainable than before. The more affordable US guitars were accordingly popular, but usually lacked the degree of charisma, quality and famous-artist associations of Fender.

The fact that this brand was already the clear leader in the UK was directly attributable to the success of Cliff and The Shadows. The influence they exerted during the early 1960s, both in their homeland and in many other countries outside America, should not be under-estimated, although it tends to be overshadowed by the Beatles-led beat group boom which followed. For a while it seemed that every player wanted a red Strat. But for many it cost well over six months' wages, and so they had to settle for something more finance-friendly. It was this economically-induced void that guitar makers in Britain and elsewhere tried to fill with a succession of cost-conscious alternatives to Fender's favourite creation.

MODEL 524.
HANK MARVIN SIGNATURE (left).
MODEL 528.
SHADOW SIGNATURE (right).

BALDWIN, an American company used to selling keyboards, bought Burns in 1965 and soon began advertising their new wares to the US music trade (above).

BALDWIN joined the rush of large American corporations to buy up smaller guitar makers in the mid 1960s. Observing the boom in demand, they sensed irresistible profit potential. What they did not know, of course, was that the boom would become a slump in a few short years, and that losses and closures would replace the general euphoria. Having bid unsuccessfully for Fender, Baldwin bought the vastly cheaper Burns set-up in 1965. Burns had already toyed with US collaborators, badging some models with the Ampeg brand, and enjoying low-key distribution by Lipsky. But the Baldwin deal quickly soured – despite glorious spirit-of-the-times publicity (left) – and the operation ceased in 1970.

BALDWIN

▽ WATKINS RAPIER 33
Produced c1961-1965 (this style); this example c1964

The average British guitarist of the decade was more likely to be saddled with something like the cheap Rapier, a stalwart of the

WEM

early 1960s beat-group scene. Charlie Watkins' London-based company was also well known for decent, low-priced amplifiers, and any British group member of the time will remember the stylish WEM logo (inset here), the initials standing for Watkins Electric Music. Toward the end of the decade Watkins used the Wilson brandname.

WATKINS did venture a little more up-market, leaning on amp expertise for models such as the Circuit 4 (left).

PRESENTING THE LATEST CONCEPT IN MODERN SOUND • PERFORMANCE AND LASTING QUALITY, COMBINED WITH A CIRCUITRY SYSTEM UNIQUE IN ITS COMBINATION OF TONE & OUTPUT

CIRCUIT 4 BY WATKINS
47 GNS WATKINS
CRAFTSMANSHIP IN SOUND

German maker Höfner had long since capitalised on Gibson's popular concept of thinline semi-acoustic guitars, but the twin-cutaway Verithin, launched in 1960, targeted this market in a more obvious manner. Höfner's small-bodied Club semis remained popular during the early part of the decade, and the company managed to stay in the solid fray by replacing earlier Gibson-derived influences with distinctly Fender-ish features and styling. The Strat was an initial inspiration, and a variation on this theme provided the basis for the popular Galaxie, bedecked with switches and roller controls. The Jazzmaster outline later found favour too, and the shape also proved popular with the other significant German maker, Framus, who used it on a succession of solids, again adorned with complex control layouts. Fellow rivals Hopf and Klira followed a similar course, and the use of multiple slide switches, rollers and rotary selectors typified the German approach to the electric guitar of the 1960s.

In Britain, the Futurama brand had originally appeared on Czech-made guitars, but these were now succeeded by instruments of Swedish origin which more faithfully followed in Fender's footsteps. These second-wave Futuramas were produced by Hagström, a company hitherto best known for accordions and similarly sparkle-finished electric guitars, but whose successful switch from squeeze-box to Strat styling was yet another sign of Fender's ever-spreading dominance.

In Italy, too, numerous accordion makers such as Eko, Crucianelli and Galanti saw that the electric guitar was the coming thing and got in on the act. Like Hagström, they opted not to abandon their heritage, and early efforts were outfitted with an abundance of sparkle and pearl plastic. Many based their creations on the Jazzmaster rather than the Strat, while others, such as Wandre, had very original ideas regarding guitar design, some quite bizarre and works of art rather than tools of the electric revolution.

Watkins, Vox and Burns were the most prominent and prolific makers in Britain. All three enjoyed quite a healthy export record to back up national sales of instruments which represented the best that the UK could offer. At the start of the

1960s Watkins began producing guitars to partner their popular budget-price small amps. The instruments trod similar territory, the Rapier model becoming a successful mainstay for many Marvin maybes.

Vox too already enjoyed amp success but the 1960s saw them add electric guitars, from entry-level planks up to ostensible alternatives to America's best. The top models initially came in Fender-inspired form, but later Vox explored less obvious avenues, resulting in the angular Phantom and the equally distinctive teardrop-shaped Mark (or 'Mk') models, perfectly capturing 1960s adventurousness.

By the start of the decade maverick maker Jim Burns had set up his own company, and typically chose to tread a decidedly different path, although Fender influences became increasingly apparent through commercial necessity. Regardless of their sometimes over-complex design quirks, Burns instruments tended to be superior in construction and components to most British-made competition. Some were aimed at first-time buyers; others at discerning players, promoted as ultimate instruments – or at least as high quality stepping stones.

In 1964 The Shadows surprisingly switched to Burns instruments, strapping on a smart set of matching models which combined Fender-derived features with original ideas. It was quite a coup for the company, although by now both band

1962

and brand were beginning to feel the impact of change – in the music, those who made it, and the tools the players chose for their ever-evolving trade. The days of matching suits and stage movements were numbered, and the time when a group deliberately sported an identical array of instruments was certainly at an end, principally thanks to The Beatles.

By the mid 1960s pop music and the electric guitar had become a virtually global partnership, and this ever-growing appeal had encouraged makers everywhere to jump on an already burgeoning bandwagon. The fruits of their labours sometimes filtered through to the UK courtesy of an enthusiastic importer or two. This meant the appearance of Matons from Australia, Musimas from East Germany and Egmonds from Holland, to name just a few. Japanese-made imports actually dwindled in the face of the increasing numbers coming from elsewhere, and this position wouldn't change until much later in the decade.

Whatever the source, the underlying motive was to satisfy a seemingly undiminished demand, and to meet it with anything even remotely resembling the real thing. Many players were far from discerning

Maton

or knowledgeable, so indifferent quality and gimmicky ideas were fostered and allowed to flourish, often ably assisted by adroit marketing. As the 1960s progressed there was a growing emphasis on playing ability and an accompanying awareness of what constituted a good guitar in terms of design and performance.

Most of the new guitar heroes of this era were from blues-based rather than pure pop backgrounds – high-powered players such as Eric Clapton and Jeff Beck. Their misuse of a Gibson Les Paul through a hard-pressed valve (tube) amp gave birth to a new sound that soon became de rigueur for many followers desperate to emulate the whining sustain that such a combination produced. The Strat's popularity faltered, until given a boost by the fiery fingers of Jimi Hendrix. Whether favouring Gibson or Fender, British players now focused squarely on American instruments, and so those from UK makers and elsewhere were increasingly left out in the cold and out of touch with guitarists' evolving demands.

Of the original British 'big three', Watkins seemed least affected by such market vagaries, content to stay within and supply a small but established niche. While the brandname varied (Watkins, Wilson,

WEM) the company's commitment to the lower end of the market remained constant, despite a few excursions into slightly higher-priced realms. Burns had been bought in 1965 by the US Baldwin Piano & Organ company. Apart from the change of name and a rationalised line, it was business as usual in Britain, which meant a diminishing share of both home and export markets. Baldwin showed little real interest or incentive to stop the rot, preferring to concentrate on consolidating their keyboards, and they called a halt to all guitar production just five years later.

Like Burns, Vox had enjoyed success in the first half of the 1960s, enough to cause problems regarding supply and demand. So they enlisted the aid of a major Italian maker, Eko, to help with manufacturing. Initially this was on a shared basis, but by the latter part of the decade all production had been switched to sunny Italy. While the American Vox guitar catalogue contained numerous novelty items, the line in Britain was more compact and conservative, although it did include the Guitar Organ and a spin-off active electronics package offered as an option on certain high-end models. But by now the company was also feeling the cold wind of change, and even Vox amplification was struggling to maintain its once-prominent position. The future of the guitars looked

△ WANDRE ROCK OVAL
Produced c1962-1963; this example c1962

No Fender knock-offs for Italian designer Wandre Pelotti; instead, an inspired piece of pure guitar sculpture that enjoyed surprisingly wide distribution (versions appeared in the US with the Noble brandname) if not widespread acceptance – although Bob Dylan can be seen eyeballing one in a London music shop with obvious interest in the 1967 on-the-road movie Don't Look Back. Not only was the body shape ahead of its time, but the guitar also features Wandre's aluminium through-neck system.

FRAMUS built solidbody (see Strato below) and thinline models (such as the Fretjet) that fired the music of many a budding 1960s Euro star. But their more esoteric archtop models included the Attila Zoller (right), named for the Bosnian jazz guitarist who lived in New York in the 1960s.

△ FRAMUS STRATO DELUXE 5/168
Produced c1962-1968; this example 1965

Fender's "offset-waist" body shape informed the designs of many European guitars, including this German Framus. The small bent handle below the bridge controls an organ-like "swell" effect.

ITALIAN electric guitars of the 1960s, with brands such as Crucianelli, Bartolini and Gemelli (right), often appear gloriously free of the usual range of design influences. Instead they seem to combine elements of espresso machines, accordions and motor-scooters with wonderfully idiosyncratic results. The Gemelli model on this catalogue cover (right) is the Twins, a typically demented piece of work with baby twins crawling over the body. Clearly, this was not a Fender copy.

decidedly dim and by the end of the decade the line had dwindled to a few Italian- and Japanese-made models.

The latter constituted an early portent of things to come, as the Japanese began to perceive the commercial potential of providing very affordable copies of currently popular electrics. Previous Far-Eastern production policy had been to incorporate only the influences of classic designs and to suggest their sources in approximate rather than exact terms. Now, however, more overt mimicry made commercial sense: the era of the 'copy guitar' had begun. In Britain the Rose-Morris company provided some of the earliest examples of this new trend, under their own Shaftesbury brand. These included Gibson and Rickenbacker lookalikes, ironic in view of Rose-Morris's previous role as Rickenbacker's UK distributor.

With no new UK makers to take the place of Burns or Vox, the market for home-grown guitars had undergone a significant shift in the 1960s, having begun the decade so optimistically in terms of demand, design and sales, but finishing up as a commercial calamity. The majority of British guitarists undoubtedly preferred to play Uncle Sam's instruments. This loyalty proved to be so established and unswerving that the British guitar-building industry would never be the same again. ■ PAUL DAY

NELSON MANDELA is jailed in South Africa. In 1964 the leader of the banned African National Congress gets a life sentence for treason resulting in his internment until 1990.

SPIDERMAN appears in Marvel comics for the first time, and becomes their most famous hero. The Beatles appear on Parlophone Records for the first time as 'Love Me Do' is released in October. They will become quite famous too.

TELSTAR, a communications satellite, is launched. It enables the first live TV transmissions between Europe and the US.

EKO was a big Italian guitar manufacturer of the 1960s, available throughout Europe, and in the US via Lo Duca. Bearing clear evidence of the company's accordion-making heritage, models such as the 700 (far left) featured typical heat-moulded plastic finishes and multiple control layouts.

JAMES BOND appears on film for the first time in Doctor No. The British secret service agent is portrayed by Sean Connery; the twangy guitar of the Bond theme tune is played by Vic Flick of The John Barry Seven.

JAMES MEREDITH enrols as the first black student at the University of Mississippi, despite riots by white students.

THUMBS CARLLILE

all thumbs

PHILIPS

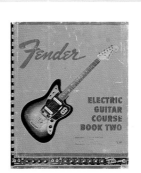

FENDER's Jaguar came in standard sunburst (above) at $379.50 in 1962, or in blond or custom colour at $398.49 (plus gold-plated hardware, $456.88).

RADIO & TELEVISION

If the progress of the 20th century has a crossroads, it occurred in the 1960s, for it was during that heady decade that the international electronic experience emerged. For guitar lovers, their instrument finally triumphed as the voice of contemporary music. This victory was inseparably tied to the growing importance of radio and TV, as people around the world increasingly tuned in and joined Marshall McLuhan's "global village".

In the United States, the path to the guitar's pre-eminence was not always a smooth one. Indeed, as the decade began, it seemed as though the guitar was losing ground. In the 1950s rock'n'roll had breathed new life into AM radio – and into

△ FENDER JAGUAR

Produced 1962-1975, reissued 1986; this example 1966

Fender's first new electric model of the 1960s was the top-of-the-line Jaguar, bearing the same offset-waist body shape as the earlier Jazzmaster. It was the first Fender with 22 frets, on a shorter-than-normal 24" scale. But the general impression was that Fender piled too many of the wrong features on the Jaguar, and the guitar has always languished in the shadow of the Strat.

guitar playing. But by 1960 a bunch of rock's rising stars were dead, including Buddy Holly and Eddie Cochran. And what's more, Little Richard had got religion, Chuck Berry was in the slammer, and Elvis was in the army.

American pop radio faced a crisis of major proportions. During 1960 AM radio was rocked with the infamous payola scandals, where DJs had accepted money and gifts to promote specific records. Among those brought down by the scandal was Alan Freed, the man most known for promoting the new guitar-driven music in the 1950s.

Instead of rock, AM airwaves in the early 1960s were filled with mostly vocal-oriented pop. Guitars weren't totally absent from the radio, of course, but most continued 1950s traditions of instrumental pop or country. Guitars on American television continued pretty much in the same vein as in the 1950s. Programming was dominated by dramas, particularly Westerns, with a growing number of situation comedies (or 'sit-coms', such as *Leave It To Beaver)* joining the blend of musical variety and game shows.

While Marshall Dillon, Adam, Hoss and Little Joe ruled the screen, guitar lovers continued to enjoy weekly 'rock videos' by Ricky Nelson, backed by Tele ace James Burton, on *The Adventures of Ozzie and Harriet,* and the smiling picking of Buddy Merrill on *The Lawrence Welk Show,* both holdovers from

the 1950s. Even brush-cut comedian Gary Moore frequently ended his show plunking amateurishly on a guitar singing a novelty song. Guitars also showed up on variety shows such as the evergreen *Ed Sullivan Show,* and the *Ford Show Starring Tennessee Ernie Ford* where top country players were often showcased. Perhaps more importantly, teens got to tune in a weekly dance party hosted by Dick Clark which, while not boasting too many guitars, at least featured the music that would become the guitar's main vehicle.

TV soundtracks often had plenty to interest the guitar fan. Scored and performed by top LA studio musicians, they were loaded with memorable melodies and guitar riffs. Players such as Laurindo Almeida, Bob Bain and Al Hendrickson routinely contributed guitar parts, but no one more than Tommy

Tedesco, whose chops were heard by millions on shows such as *Bonanza, Gunsmoke, Rawhide, Maverick, Have Gun Will Travel, The Rifleman, Wagon Train, Route 66* and countless other classic TV shows as well as movies from the decade.

Significantly, one other place guitars did show up on American TV was the vapid *The Many Loves of Dobie Gillis* (1959-63), a sit-com which parodied late-1950s beatniks and in which Gillis constantly fled homely Zelda Gilroy and tried to learn how to play guitar. The guitar in the corner was a sign of what was to come: the folk revival that would indicate the first signs of the 1960s guitar boom.

The impact of folk music was felt almost immediately on both TV and radio. Catching the trend, in 1961 the prolific Columbia record producer Mitch Miller successfully translated his popular, saccharine choral singalong records of folk music onto the small screen with *Sing Along With Mitch.* While this had more to do with bouncing balls than guitars, it did serve to reassure parents that the folk music their kids were playing on guitar was safe and healthy. Little did they know.

Radio stations also quickly caught the wave, and chart success of the more commercial folk singers, as well as Mitch Miller, finally did bring guitar to the fore on TV with *Hootenanny* (1963-64), an artificial recreation of popular college events featuring acts such as The Smothers Brothers,

DUANE EDDY ROCK 'N ROLL GUITARS

DUANE EDDY (left) fired most of his twangy instrumentals with a Gretsch 6120, but used a Guild "signature" model on stage for a while in the 1960s.

▽ GUILD DUANE EDDY
Produced 1962-c1969; this example 1962

Based in New Jersey, the Guild company had a reputation for making fine jazz-style archtop acoustic and electric guitars, but tried to entice 1960s rockers with this Duane Eddy model. The guitar shown here belongs to Duane "Twang" Eddy himself.

AT VALCO a worker (right) adjusts a mould for a plastic body, while (far right) president Robert Engelhardt (left) and engineer Walter Churchill check a finished guitar.

△ NATIONAL NEWPORT 84
Produced 1962-1965 (also Val-Pro 84);
this example c1964

Valco was never short of impressive names for its guitar innovations, marketed mainly with National or Supro brands. These new fibreglass-body guitars were no exception: "Res-O-Glas" and "Hollow-Glas" appeared in Valco catalogues and ads to describe the material used in its new line of National non-wood instruments. In fact, the bodies were made from fibreglass-reinforced polyster, which Valco thought would provide a longer-lasting guitar. But this brave and stylish plastic experiment ended with Valco itself in the late 1960s.

READY, Steady, Go! was the hippest British pop TV programme of the 1960s, beamed into millions of homes on a Friday evening ("the weekend starts here") from a Swinging London studio, at first with Manfred Mann's '5-4-3-2-1' as its theme. It featured all the right groups – seen in action here (right) are regular guests The Kinks – but incidentally showcased the right clothes, the right dances and the right atmosphere. Unusually, RSG stopped at its peak, lasting for just three years after its debut in 1963.

Josh White and The Carter Family, all sporting guitars. The idealism of the folk revival quickly yielded to a stark intrusion of a darker reality. Within minutes of President Kennedy's assassination in Dallas, Texas, in November 1963, moving pictures of the event floated over TVs. Viewers in the US and, thanks to the newly-launched communications satellite Telstar, around the world were transfixed in heart-stopping horror and grief. Never before had an entire population watched real-life tragedy – which would include the killing of Kennedy's accused assassin – unfold live on the tube. Innocence had come face-to-face with experience.

The Kennedy assassination was significant because it was a culmination of changes that had been creeping into the artificiality of TV-land, asserting reality in the form of news reportage. Slowly but surely world events were coming into American living rooms via the TV set, from Gary Powers' U-2 spy plane incident in 1960 through 1962's near-apocalyptic Cuban missile crisis. For the rest of the decade, news would become an increasingly vital function of television, the most

significant being the reports of the growing military involvement in Vietnam.

Only weeks after the Kennedy assassination came the British Invasion of the US. At 8pm on Sunday, February 9th 1964, just after *My Favorite Martian,* The Beatles took the stage on *The Ed Sullivan Show* (though they'd actually been seen on American TV a month earlier in a film clip on the Jack Paar show). The Beatles' subsequent concerts caused near riots, and made newscasts across the country. Almost immediately

the American airwaves bristled with British accents. The contrast between US hits of the early 1960s and 1964 is amazing: ten top hits by The Beatles, two by The Rolling Stones, plus The Animals' 'House Of The Rising Sun' and The Kinks' 'You Really Got Me', all British and all drenched in classic guitar licks.

Pop television in Britain in the 1960s didn't get any better than *Ready, Steady, Go!* which began in August 1963. The show was a mirror to the beat boom, reproducing the feel of

NATIONAL first appeared as an independent brand in the 1920s, but by the 1960s was part of the renamed Chicago-based Valco Manufacturing company. The best-known National instruments of the 1960s are the plastic- and wood-body "map shape" guitars, so-called because the body outline is supposed to resemble part of a map of the United States. The entirely un-famous Kim Sisters model a couple of map-shape Nationals in this 1966 ad (far right). As well as its more outrageous designs, Valco also produced many more conventional models, as this contemporary catalogue (right) shows. Valco bought the Kay guitar company in 1967, but unfortunately when Kay went out of business during the following year they took Valco with them.

▽ SILVERTONE 1457 GUITAR/AMP/CASE SET
Produced 1962-1967; this example c1964

A brilliant idea by the Danelectro company of New Jersey – marketed by Sears under its Silvertone brandname – was this guitar that came with a case (below) that had a built-in amplifier.

SILVERTONE's ingenious "all-in-one" outfit boasted a guitar case with built-in amplifier and speaker. "One easy-to-carry unit," said Sears' publicity, which offered the two-pickup guitar and tremolo-amp cased set for just $99.95.

ED SULLIVAN (right) presented all the top bands of the 1960s on his TV show.

a club gig in a London TV studio and featuring all the best new pop acts as well as a hip American visitor or two. It was required viewing for fledgling guitarists who could ogle a procession of rare delights from Gretsch, Vox, Rickenbacker, Höfner, Gibson, Burns, Fender and more. The show's presenters included Cathy McGowan and Keith Fordyce. With McGowan, it was as if one of the avowedly hip audience had been given a microphone seconds before the show went on air. But the avuncular Fordyce remembers that during its brief three-year run *Ready, Steady, Go!* had its finger firmly on the musical pulse: "It perfectly reflected the rising British pop scene of the time, and as an utterly contemporary news magazine it was compelling to watch. It told you exactly what was happening in terms of dress and music and people." In contrast to this commercial TV offering, the BBC had two key shows. *Juke Box Jury* boasted a panel of stars voting new records a hit (ding!) or a miss (bzzz), famously including all four Beatles in 1963 seen by an audience of 24 million viewers, not far short of half Britain's population. *Top Of The Pops* debuted in 1964 and is still going strong today with its shameless rundown of chart hits that culminates with the week's number one single.

Radio in Britain in the first few years of the 1960s meant the BBC, where the broadcast of records ('needle time') was limited by an agreement with the Musicians' Union designed to increase work for musicians. This meant that sessions by pop groups, specially recorded at BBC studios, were put out on BBC stations throughout the decade, providing many players with their first taste of 'proper' recording as well as an early and often important connection with their potential audience. Auditions were held for these sessions – The Beatles, for example, still with Pete Best on drums, passed their BBC radio audition in February 1962 and made their first broadcast the following month, the first opportunity that most people outside Liverpool had to hear the group. Every top British group, and a whole army of lesser-known acts, recorded sessions at the BBC, and for some it was a stepping stone to success. Guitarist Dave Edmunds of Love Sculpture, for example, recalled the run-up to 'Sabre Dance' in 1968: "We did a live session for [DJ] John Peel's *Top Gear,* and suddenly we were signed up by EMI... and we had a number two single," said Edmunds.

The down side of the 'needle time' agreement was that record companies found it difficult to get their wares broadcast over the airwaves in Britain. Radio Luxembourg did play pop records, and thousands of British teenagers would tune in to the distant station when it could be received at night, just to hear the rare music amid the static. Record plugger Ronan O'Rahilly, frustrated at the lack of outlets for his clients, decided in 1964 to begin broadcasts a little closer to Britain,

ERIC CLAPTON (right) plays his Gibson ES-335 (see also below) at London's Royal Albert Hall in November 1968 during Cream's farewell tour – later portrayed in the Farewell Cream film. Three songs from an earlier show at The Forum in Los Angeles turned up on the Goodbye Cream LP.

△ GIBSON ES-335TDC

Produced 1962-1982 (this style); this example May 1964

This Gibson 335 is owned by Eric Clapton. He bought it in the 1960s and first used it toward the end of Cream's brief if illustrious career, most notably on the group's "farewell" concerts during late 1968 in Los Angeles, San Diego and London. While Clapton's SG (see p.48-49) was his favoured studio guitar at the time, this 335 may have been the guitar he used to record 'Badge' in 1968. The guitar's original case, complete with CREAM stencil, is pictured above. Gibson's 335, a 1950s design, reached new heights of popularity in the 1960s.

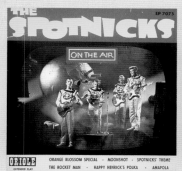

THE SPOTNICKS (far left) were a clearly unhinged Swedish guitar group whose deranged gimmick was to appear on stage in spacesuits. When a cinema version was made of the TV show

Thunderbirds (centre), puppets of The Shadows were featured, complete with tiny Burns guitars. The Monkees (left) started on TV as puppets of a rather different kind, but slowly established their own identities.

stations, creating a market for chart hits by The Doors, Jefferson Airplane and a host of less commercial classics by Quicksilver Messenger Service, The Grateful Dead, Blue Cheer, Canned Heat, Big Brother & The Holding Company and others. By 1968 most American cities of significant size boasted FM underground radio stations, and by the end of 1969 around 75 per cent of households in larger markets had FM radios.

One of the most inventive years for guitar-led music was 1967, with a soundtrack provided by the likes of Traffic, Buffalo Springfield, Vanilla Fudge, Creedence Clearwater Revival, Steppenwolf, Cream, and Iron Butterfly's lengthy 'In-A-Gadda-Da-Vida'. The Beatles appeared on the decade's most celebrated approximation of the electronic global village, *Our World,* an international TV link-up in which Britain was represented by The Fabs in a hippie-infested summer-of-love studio singing and strumming along to 'All You Need Is Love'.

Guitars continued to be influential for the rest of the 1960s, but by 1968 the decade had already begun to unravel. Indeed, it was in '68 that the bottom fell out of the fabled guitar boom, claiming Valco/Kay and many foreign manufacturers as victims. The Martin Luther King and Robert Kennedy assassinations punctuated US news reports of escalating violence both in south-east Asia and back home in the streets. On television this turmoil was reflected in *The Smothers Brothers Comedy Hour,* wherein the amusing pickers (Tom on a Guild) featured anti-war performers and heavy social satire. Almost as counterpoint, and as a caricature of The Beatles' cartoon series which had been running (with actors voices) since 1965, promoter Don Kirshner

introduced *The Archies* rock cartoon, creating 'bubblegum' rock. What emerged from the 1960s was the transformation of the modern media. While it would take another decade or so to complete, in the United States underground FM radio had pushed AM radio down the slippery slope into irrelevance, while television had crossed over from being almost purely entertainment to becoming the medium of, for better or worse,

a new reality. In Britain, the importance of pop music was recognised and tolerated by the broadcasting establishment. And while one could trace the progress back a long way, the guitar had finally and without doubt become established as *the* pop music icon. In December 1969, Led Zeppelin's 'Whole Lotta Love' hit number one in the US singles charts, and the 1970s had begun. ■ MICHAEL WRIGHT

FENDER was bought by the Columbia Broadcast System Inc – better known as CBS – in 1965, and as this wonderfully evocative shot from Fender's 1969 catalogue shows the parent company was not slow to underline the guitar-maker's connection to one of America's leading TV companies. Guitars and television were central to American culture in the 1960s, and it was in front of CBS cameras (and alongside presenter Ed Sullivan) that The Beatles' invasion of the States commenced in 1964.

▽ GRETSCH PRINCESS
Produced 1962-1963; this example 1962

"THE FIRST time that an instrument has been selectively constructed for girls," drooled the Gretsch publicity boys. But the Princess failed to fool the girls and faded fast from public view.

△ GRETSCH WHITE FALCON STEREO
Produced 1962-1981 (this style); this example 1966

Gretsch followed the pattern set by Gibson, and during 1961 and 1962 changed the design of their leading hollow electric models, including the fabulous White Falcon, to a twin-cutaway style.

GRETSCH launched several solidbody guitars during the 1960s. The Corvette (pictured, near left, in 1965 catalogue) was also redecorated to provide the pastel Princess and striped-pickguard Twist models. The bizarre Astro-Jet (far left) was claimed by Gretsch to be "as bold and challenging as the modern world we live in".

What's New
and Exciting in Solid Bodies?
Firebird Guitars and Thunderbird Basses by Gibson

Chances are, you *show* solid body models to a large percentage of your guitar customers. After all, the new sound of today's music depends upon them for its distinctive beat.

Chances are, you will *sell* more of these customers when you show them the new Firebird by Gibson. Revolutionary in shape, sound, *and colors*, the new Firebird is sure to create sales excitement through customer preference. Its fresh and daring design . . . its brilliant, solid sound match the needs of the musicians who play today's music. Models with one, two, or three pickups are available in ten custom colors."

Equally exciting is the Thunderbird bass with single or double pickup. And, the Gibson price range—$199.50 to $470.00—clinches sales to the amateur, semi-pro, and professional performer.

Gibson
KALAMAZOO, MICHIGAN

GIBSON *started the 1960s determined to take on their chief rival Fender, designing the Firebird guitar and Thunderbird bass (1964 ad, left) with clear recognition of the solidbody style of the West Coast firm. But it didn't work, and Gibson's 1960s sales had to rely on classic 1950s designs such as the semi-solid ES-335.*

and the showmanship of custom color

Choose the color you want . . . to enhance your performance

GIBSON *not only aped Fender design with the Firebirds, but borrowed their custom colour idea too, applying car paints to guitars. One Gibson colour (Golden Mist) was actually identical to a Fender colour (Shoreline Gold). Gibson used its Oldsmobile name; Fender applied the Pontiac term.*

△ GIBSON FIREBIRD V
Produced 1963-1965 (this style); this example August 1965

Despite the novel sculpting of the SG design that Gibson had introduced at the start of the decade, the company still found its guitar styles compared unfavourably to those of Fender. So they brought in an automobile designer, Ray Dietrich, who was asked to out-Fender Fender. The result was the Firebird series, launched in 1963. This one is finished in Gibson's Cardinal Red.

△ GIBSON FIREBIRD I
Produced 1965-1969 (this style); this example December 1965

BRIAN JONES (left) was often seen in the mid-1960s with this attractive sunburst Firebird VII, but not even an unofficial endorsement from a Rolling Stone was enough to give Gibson the sales boost it wanted from its stylish Firebird models.

Gibson's attempt to modernise its line with the Firebirds faltered: sales were poor, and Fender complained about similarities to its patented body features. So the original Firebird design – known now as the "reverse" body – was dropped in 1965. Gibson revamped the series with this new shape – the "non-reverse" body – and dropped the more expensive neck-through-body construction in favour of Gibson's usual glued neck. Still unsuccessful, the Firebirds were grounded for good during 1969.

GIBSON GUITARS

For Gibson the 1960s began as an extension of the highly creative 1950s period which had seen the coming of age of the electric guitar. There were more new models, and record sales, thanks to the success of musical styles ubiquitously supported by the guitar. Midway through the decade, however, the company seemed to lose its flair for innovation... but fortunately at a time when the Les Paul design from the 1950s was reintroduced as a result of enormous popular demand.

On the threshold of the 1960s Gibson was a leading contender in the field of professional-grade electric guitars. Unlike most other US makers the company boasted a full line of electrics, ranging from traditional archtops to solidbodies through semi-solid thinlines, as well as basses and electrified flat-tops like the J-160E. Gibson, however, was no longer the dominant player it had been. Several brands – some old like Gretsch, others more recent like Fender – were actively challenging its electric franchise. Competition is what prompted Gibson to start the 1960s by

dropping the sunburst Les Paul Standard, widely acknowledged today as the most desirable solidbody guitar ever. At the time, though, a lightweight body with more aggressive styling and full access to the neck seemed necessary to rekindle the Les Paul Standard's flagging market appeal. With guitars increasingly used as solo instruments, players wanted to be able to play easily in the higher registers to expand their tonal range, and a double cutaway body was the answer. The first samples of the revamped Les Paul Standard came out in late 1960 showcasing an innovative double cutaway with pointed horns, highly bevelled edges and an ultra-thin rim. Another sign of the times: the new model was the first Gibson marketed with a vibrato tailpiece as a regular built-in appointment.

By 1961 the novel body shape was gradually adopted by the other solidbody variants (Custom, Junior, Special, TV) in lieu of their previous slab-body designs, whether single or double cutaway. At the end of 1962 it was applied in an elongated form to the custom-made double necks, and eventually, in 1966, it would serve for the final restyling of the low-end Melody Maker series.

Meanwhile the Les Paul markings were dropped in late 1963 and the Standard, Custom and Junior were simply called 'SG', for Solid Guitar (not Sixties Guitar). The reasons behind this removal have nothing to do with the fact that Les Paul did

not like the sculptured SG design. The wizard of Waukesha chose not to renew his endorsement contract because of his ongoing divorce with Mary Ford – he did not want money coming in that might be made part of the settlement. By coincidence, 1963 is also the year when shipments of Gibson acoustics began to exceed those of electrics for the first time since 1954, a situation that would continue during the rest of the 1960s. ('Shipment' is the official term for the number of particular guitars that left the Gibson factory.)

Making playing more comfortable in the upper register was desirable not just on solidbodies. At the end of 1960 a deep 'Florentine' cutaway was introduced on the archtop electrics that had a 17"-wide body. The pointed horn became the hallmark of the Super 400CES, L-5CES and Byrdland of the decade, since the arguably more graceful round cutaway was not reinstated until 1969.

However, Gibson's major effort in its traditional area was the release of Artist models endorsed by Barney Kessel, Johnny Smith and Tal Farlow. All of them were great guitarists, but they were 1950s jazzers in a period which would eventually be dominated by folk, pop and rock music. The artist rostrum was later completed with Trini Lopez, a nightclub act who would be the farthest Gibson would ever go in recruiting a pop endorser for a model during the 1960s (except of course The Everly Brothers on the acoustic side). Later in the decade, though,

RADIO CAROLINE (right) was the best-known of a number of British "pirate" radio stations of the 1960s. But the popularity of so much illegal activity proved too testing for the authorities, who banned the pirates in 1967. Instead, the BBC's new Radio One station was inaugurated.

from a ship called Caroline anchored off the Sussex coast. Radio Caroline prompted others, including Radio London, and pirate radio poured forth, playing non-stop all the guitar-soaked pop records that the BBC could not, and introducing DJs such as John Peel, Kenny Everett and Tony Blackburn. Officialdom finally caught up with the pirates, and in 1967 the Marine Offences Act put a stop to them. Later the same year the BBC began its new pop station, Radio One... which had the brilliant idea of employing DJs such as John Peel, Kenny Everett and Tony Blackburn.

Back in the US, the impact of the British Invasion had been felt almost instantaneously on TV in 1964, as the turtlenecked acoustic pickers of *Hootenanny* were promptly replaced by the electric picking and go-go dancing of ABC's *Shindig* (in black-and-white) and the following year by NBC's *Hullabaloo* (in colour) whose guests included the Stones (with Brian Jones introducing Vox 'teardrop' guitars to American audiences), The Beatles, Glen Campbell and (a liberated) Chuck Berry. Even the venerable Dick Clark launched a weekly rock variety show in 1965 called *Where The Action Is,* prominently featuring the sight and sound of Epiphone-toting Seattle-based band Paul Revere & The Raiders.

Hollywood created its own TV-land version of The Beatles in 1966, The Monkees. Even though two members were musicians, following the old form none got to play on their early shows or records; Tommy Tedesco and others did. Meanwhile, as body counts and student protests increasingly got the attention of the media, so did drugs. Most of the new psychedelic rock groups sprang from local clubs – without the support of major record labels, who were still seeking commercial pop bands with sub-three-minute songs for AM radio – and so became known as 'underground'. This music not only elevated the importance of guitar solos in pop music, but had a far more significant impact on the media in that it virtually created the ultimate success of FM radio.

FM radio had been invented in 1933 by E.H. Armstrong. Unlike AM radio which transmits by varying the height of sound waves ('amplitude modulation'), FM varies the intervals between sound waves ('frequency modulation') and yields much better quality. The first FM stations were licensed in 1943, despite resistance from networks and record companies which had a huge investment in AM technology. During the 1950s, FM radio had been nicknamed 'Fine Music' because with its longer selections and fewer interruptions it suited classical and MOR 'elevator' music. Selling this to advertisers in the US was tough, and growth was slow, even with the introduction of FM stereo in 1962.

FM became a perfect outlet for the new underground music, which was generally denied access to AM radio. In 1967 San Francisco's KMPX became one of the first underground radio

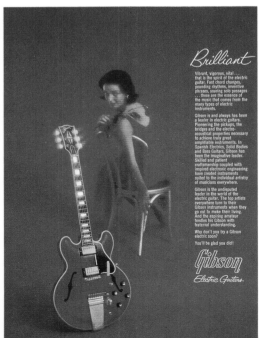

GIBSON's "thinline" twin-cutaway models were a very important part of the company's line at the time, as the luxurious presentation of the ES-355 on this early-1960s catalogue shows.

REVISED Firebirds (the "non-reverse" models) included the I with two single-coil pickups, III with three single-coils, V (far right) with two mini-humbuckers, and VII (right) with three mini-humbuckers. Relaunch prices were set at $199.50 (I), $249.50 (III), $299.50 (V) and $394.50 (VII).

FIREBIRD VII
Here is the ultimate in a solid body guitar by Gibson. A completely new and exciting instrument

FIREBIRD V
Another in the revolutionary new series of solid body guitars by Gibson. Exciting in concept, excit...

△ GIBSON FIREBIRD I
Produced 1963-1965 (this style); this example April 1964

There were four original Firebird models, all fitted with mini-humbucking pickups. The I had one pickup and was the only Firebird without a vibrato; its launch price was $189.50. The III ($249.50) had two pickups and a stud bridge, the V ($325) two pickups and a tune-o-matic bridge, and the top-of-the-line VII ($445) had three pickups. Standard finish was sunburst, like the I shown here, but custom colours were offered for an extra $15.

New CORVETTE Sting Ray by Chevrolet

Today's Complete Stocks — 5 Star Final LATE SPORTS
10¢ Honolulu Star-Bulletin
KENNEDY KILLED; EX-TURNCOAT HELD
Sniper's Bullet Fells President

PRESIDENT KENNEDY is assassinated in Dallas, Texas, and Lyndon B Johnson becomes president the same day; 48 hours later Lee Harvey Oswald, accused of Kennedy's murder, is shot and killed by Jack Ruby, a nightclub owner.

DR TIMOTHY LEARY and a colleague are sacked from Harvard for experimenting on students with LSD. "Drugs," writes Norman Mailer, "are a spiritual form of gambling."

THE CORVETTE Stingray is the chic new US car. Designed by Bill Mitchell, the coupe has split windows on a "boat-tail" rear, and pivoting headlights.

GIBSON reacted to the 1960s guitar boom with apparent ease, indicative of a company that had made instruments since the turn of the century. There was luck too: a factory expansion was completed in 1961 (architect's drawing, below), doubling its size and poised for the folk boom and the Beatles boom. Gibson had used the Kalamazoo brand for cheap products since the 1930s, and in 1965 revived it (right) to feed the demand for budget

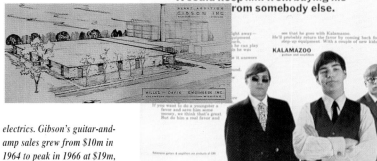

Sell Kalamazoo to a beginner buying his first guitar and amplifier. It could keep him from buying his ...rom somebody else.

electrics. Gibson's guitar-and-amp sales grew from $10m in 1964 to peak in 1966 at $19m, falling to $14m by 1969.

there would be several certified guitar heroes using Gibsons as their workhorses, not least Eric Clapton who would play a Les Paul Standard, an SG Standard, a Firebird I and an ES-335.

The beginning of the 1960s witnessed unprecedented growth for the guitar industry, often recalled as the first guitar boom. To be sure not to miss out on market opportunities, Gibson had doubled its factory floor space up to 120,000 square feet in 1961. Two further plants were acquired, in 1962 and 1964, bringing another 80,000 square feet of space dedicated to amplifiers and electronics. These huge expansions were well inspired because by 1964, the year of the British Invasion of the US spearheaded by The Beatles, most manufacturers became unable to keep up with demand.

Given such buoyant market conditions, the sales of SG-styled electrics looked good but fell short of being spectacular. Like other Gibson guitars they were not ideal for the thunderous staccato of surf music or the twang of country styles. Besides, they were essentially monochrome (red or white) and the sideways vibrato fitted to the Standard and Custom models was inappropriate, to say the least. Something else was needed, something that could encroach upon the Fender preserve in sounds and looks while displaying typical Gibson feel and workmanship. An automobile designer named Ray Dietrich was enrolled to devise a new line of solidbodies, collectively known as the Firebird

BRITAIN is rocked by scandal and crime. Conservative politician John Profumo resigns after disclosure of his involvement with Christine Keeler, mistress of a Soviet naval attaché. A gang steals an unprecedented £2.5 million from a mail train, achieved by hiding a green signal light with an old glove and lighting the red signal with torch batteries.

MARTIN LUTHER KING delivers a speech to a gathering in Washington: "I have a dream that one day this nation will rise up, live out the true meaning of its creed: we hold these truths to be self-evident, that all men are created equal." Meanwhile, 5000 are arrested on a civil rights march in Alabama as Governor George Wallace refuses to open the University there to black students.

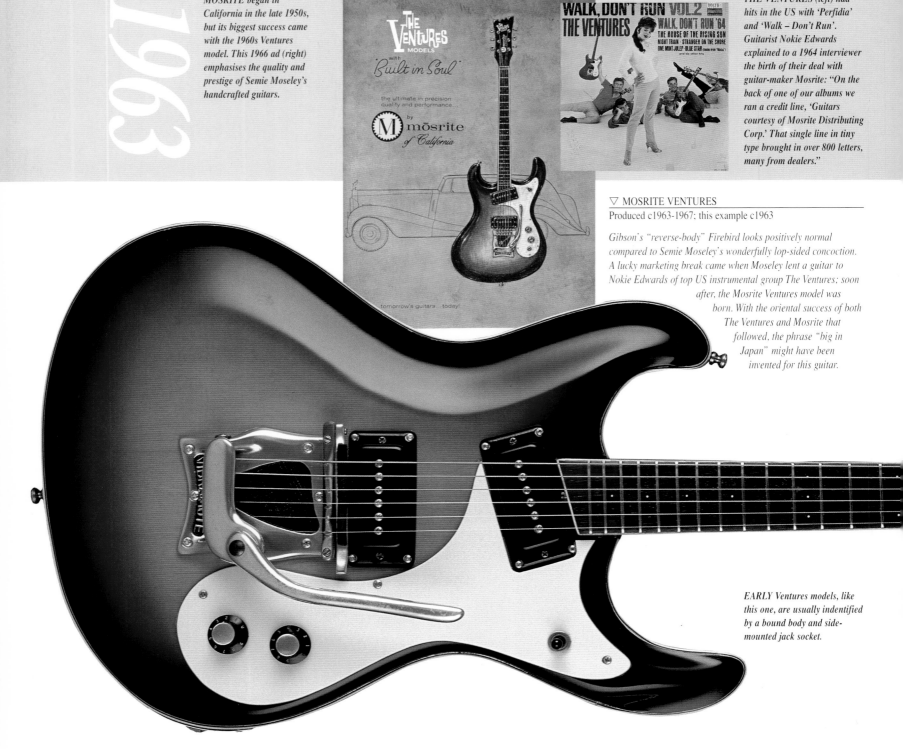

MOSRITE began in California in the late 1950s, but its biggest success came with the 1960s Ventures model. This 1966 ad (right) emphasises the quality and prestige of Semie Moseley's handcrafted guitars.

THE VENTURES
MODELS
with
Built in Soul

the ultimate in precision quality and performance...
by
M mōsrite
of California

WALK, DON'T RUN VOL2
THE VENTURES
WALK, DON'T RUN '64
THE HOUSE OF THE RISING SUN
NIGHT TRAIN · STRANGER ON THE SHORE
ONE MINT JULEP · BLUE STAR and six other hits

THE VENTURES (left) had hits in the US with 'Perfidia' and 'Walk – Don't Run'. Guitarist Nokie Edwards explained to a 1964 interviewer the birth of their deal with guitar-maker Mosrite: "On the back of one of our albums we ran a credit line, 'Guitars courtesy of Mosrite Distributing Corp.' That single line in tiny type brought in over 800 letters, many from dealers."

tomorrow's guitars... today!

▽ MOSRITE VENTURES
Produced c1963-1967; this example c1963

Gibson's "reverse-body" Firebird looks positively normal compared to Semie Moseley's wonderfully lop-sided concoction. A lucky marketing break came when Moseley lent a guitar to Nokie Edwards of top US instrumental group The Ventures; soon after, the Mosrite Ventures model was born. With the oriental success of both The Ventures and Mosrite that followed, the phrase "big in Japan" might have been invented for this guitar.

EARLY Ventures models, like this one, are usually indentified by a bound body and side-mounted jack socket.

series. No less than four guitars – the Firebird I, III, V and VII – and two Thunderbird basses were premiered in 1963. They were characterised by an asymmetrical body shape with a pronounced lower horn on the treble side and by a neck-through-body construction. The series was the first to be marketed by Gibson with ten optional custom colours, meant to emulate Fender's already well-established coloured finishes.

The 'reverse' body shape, as it's now known, could be viewed either as a smoothed-out variant of the Explorer or as the mirror image of an elongated Jazzmaster. Fender adhered to the second stance and claimed that the shape was infringing upon its patented 'offset-waist' design. The argument never reached the courts because disappointing sales led Gibson to modify the series in 1965. A second generation of Firebirds adopted a more conventional 'non-reverse' design (still kind of Fender-like) with a glued-on neck, but success remained elusive, despite the addition of a 12-string model.

Following on from the 1950s sunburst Les Paul Standard and 'Modernistic' Flying V and Explorer, the original Firebird series would become the third part in Gibson's revered trilogy of famous models now recognised as ahead of their time. But although their unique features are more widely praised today, the stylish Firebirds have remained less popular than other Gibson designs. This may be due to their pickups, as players tend to prefer regular humbuckers to the Firebird 'mini' variants (which were designed to be without adjustable polepieces).

Despite the Firebird hiccup, 1965 was a great year for Gibson marked by all-time record shipments. But by the following year the company was confronted with various problems, including how to replace its president, Ted McCarty, and its factory superintendent, John Huis. The two men had bought the Bigsby vibrato operation from Paul Bigsby, a long-time Gibson supplier. For Chicago Musical Instrument Co (CMI), Gibson's parent freshly quoted on the New York stock exchange, this was perceived as a potential conflict of interest, and consequently McCarty and Huis chose to resign rather than see Bigsby lose Gibson's business. Their departure is often considered as a watershed in Gibson's history, mainly because of the stalled creativity and the quality problems found in the ensuing period – not to mention the number of true classics

Gibson
GUITARS AND AMPLIFIERS

introduced while McCarty had steered the company from March 1948 until June 1966. Quality had indeed become a serious issue. Too many models of different types were in production, and there was a much greater output compared to the 1950s. Less efficient moisture control caused plenty of wood cracking and led to a higher reject ratio, as well as to an inordinate amount of returns under warranty. Problems involving wood supplies, equipment, personnel and unions coalesced to push back-orders into tens of thousands of dollars. This was most untimely because demand was tapering off, while a bigger share of the guitar market was falling prey to oriental manufacturers.

The second half of the 1960s saw the emergence of new trends which would persist into the next decade. Production at Gibson went through a swingeing rationalisation to make the instruments stronger and less prone to warranty work. This trend gathered plenty of momentum with Stanley Rendell,

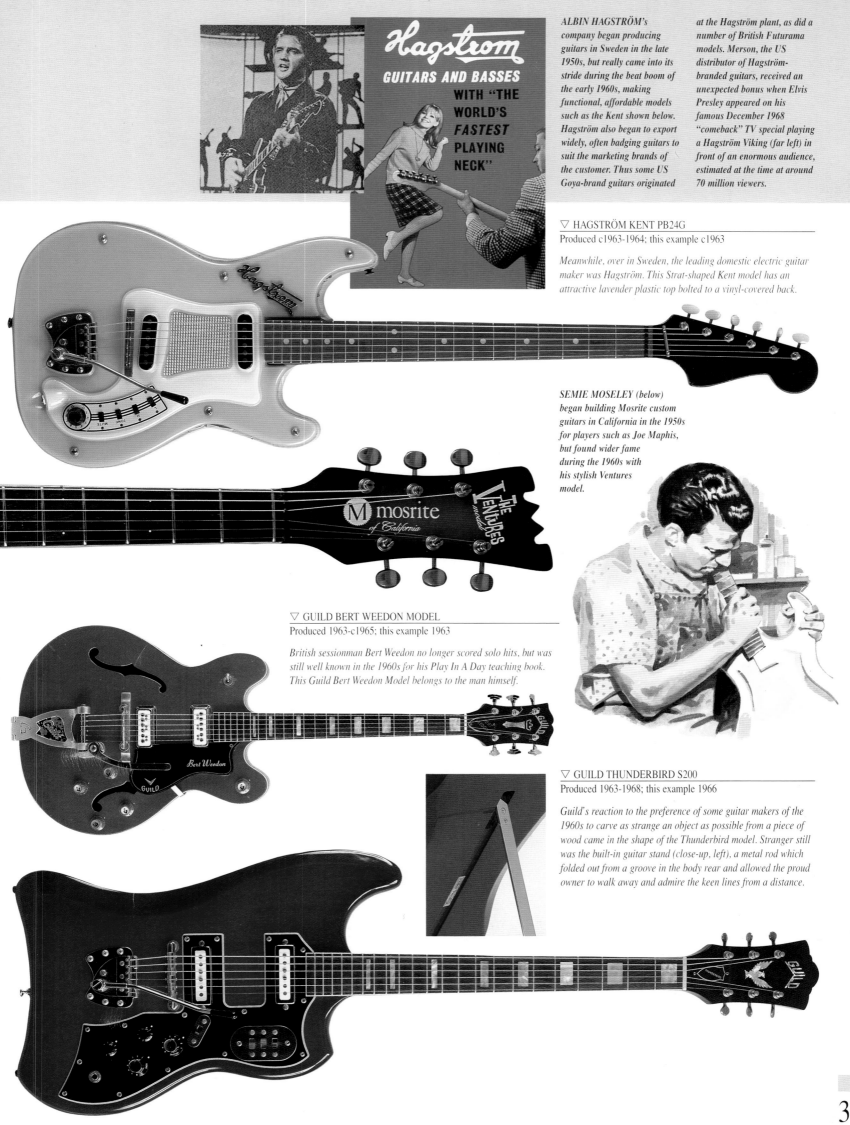

ALBIN HAGSTRÖM's company began producing guitars in Sweden in the late 1950s, but really came into its stride during the beat boom of the early 1960s, making functional, affordable models such as the Kent shown below. Hagström also began to export widely, often badging guitars to suit the marketing brands of the customer. Thus some US Goya-brand guitars originated at the Hagström plant, as did a number of British Futurama models. Merson, the US distributor of Hagström-branded guitars, received an unexpected bonus when Elvis Presley appeared on his famous December 1968 "comeback" TV special playing a Hagström Viking (far left) in front of an enormous audience, estimated at the time at around 70 million viewers.

▽ HAGSTRÖM KENT PB24G
Produced c1963-1964; this example c1963

Meanwhile, over in Sweden, the leading domestic electric guitar maker was Hagström. This Strat-shaped Kent model has an attractive lavender plastic top bolted to a vinyl-covered back.

SEMIE MOSELEY (below) began building Mosrite custom guitars in California in the 1950s for players such as Joe Maphis, but found wider fame during the 1960s with his stylish Ventures model.

▽ GUILD BERT WEEDON MODEL
Produced 1963-c1965; this example 1963

British sessionman Bert Weedon no longer scored solo hits, but was still well known in the 1960s for his Play In A Day teaching book. This Guild Bert Weedon Model belongs to the man himself.

▽ GUILD THUNDERBIRD S200
Produced 1963-1968; this example 1966

Guild's reaction to the preference of some guitar makers of the 1960s to carve as strange an object as possible from a piece of wood came in the shape of the Thunderbird model. Stranger still was the built-in guitar stand (close-up, left), a metal rod which folded out from a groove in the body rear and allowed the proud owner to walk away and admire the keen lines from a distance.

1964

▽ RICKENBACKER ASTRO AS-51
Produced 1964; this example 1964

This Rickenbacker creation was a build-it-yourself solidbody electric guitar kit aimed at the Christmas 1964 gift market, coming as an "educational and lots of fun" box of 25 parts.

ACOUSTIC 12-string guitars have been around since at least the 1930s, the idea being to make one guitar sound like at least two. Amplified – and in the right hands – the sound can be glorious, as The Byrds' 'Eight Miles High' testifies.

▷ KAWAI "AMP-IN-GUITAR"
Produced c1964-1965; this example c1964

Following the general 1960s rule that rules were there to be broken, someone wondered why the amp and speaker should be separate from the guitar. So they combined them. Although this example is brandless, the pickups suggest it was made in Japan by Kawai, and it is similar to fellow Japanese maker Teisco's more sophisticated TRG amp-in-guitar models of the period.

THE WHO established a new vitality in English pop during the 1960s. Never a great lead guitarist, Pete Townshend's skill was more to do with his ability as a rhythm player, deploying cascading chords on records such as this 1966 album A Quick One (below).

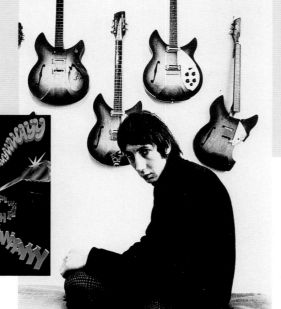

PETE TOWNSHEND (left) has explained his use of a 12-string Rickenbacker on the classic 1965 Who single 'I Can't Explain' as "a chord machine". But soon he became known just as much for the smashing time he had with his hapless guitars, and is pictured in his London flat in 1966 (left) surrounded by Ricks in various stages of dismemberment. "I sometimes feel very bad about having smashed up instruments which were particularly good ones," he said much later, "but generally I was working with production-line instruments."

▽ RICKENBACKER 330S/12 "1993"
Produced 1964-1967; this example July 1964

Although theirs was not the first electric 12-string, Rickenbacker produced the version that came to mass attention following its adoption first by George Harrison (in The Beatles) and soon afterwards by Roger McGuinn (in The Byrds). From that time on, jingle-jangle guitar nearly always meant electric Rickenbacker.

A US DESTROYER is attacked by North Vietnamese torpedo boats. President Johnson orders retaliatory air strikes, backed by Congress which in the Gulf Of Tonkin resolution authorises the president to take any steps necessary "to maintain peace".

MODS & ROCKERS go into battle at British seaside resorts. Fashionable mods take speed, drive scooters and listen to soul music. Leather-jacketed rockers drink, drive motorcycles and listen to rock'n'roll. Arbitration is not sought.

CASSIUS CLAY takes the world heavyweight boxing title. He later changes his name to Muhammad Ali.

GIBSON did not fare well in the 1960s when signing musicians to "design" guitars. Trini Lopez was an especially odd choice: he was not a guitarist's guitarist, nor was he a particularly big star ('If I Had A Hammer' was his only big hit), but Gibson still put out two Trini Lopez models, as seen in this 1965 ad (above).

appointed as Gibson's new chief in early 1968. Rendell also saw fit to restore a greater product focus by weeding out mediocre sellers, while concentrating on the more remunerative high-end models. For example, the annual shipments of the Super 400CES, the L-5CES and the Byrdland grew from, respectively, 32-44-77 in 1965 up to an unprecedented 63-200-218 by 1968. Conversely, low-end models like the one-pickup Melody Maker and SG Junior saw their totals drop from 6,753 and 3,570 in 1965 to just 338 and 561 in 1968. With plenty of cheaper imports, competition was too strong in these lower market segments.

With Gibson lacking inspiration to design new electrics, another major trend was the reintroduction of 'old' designs. The first reissue was the Flying V in 1966, but it hardly set the world on fire (despite the occasional support of Jimi Hendrix). The big coup came in 1968 with the return of the original Les Paul design. Several influential players, like Eric Clapton in the UK and Mike Bloomfield in the US, had discovered the exceptional sonic properties of 1950s Les Pauls when played at high volume. The advent of the so-called blues boom in the mid 1960s helped to create a demand that even a relatively conservative company like Gibson could not ignore. However, with the early reissues Gibson paid scant attention to details and failed to notice that the model in demand was the 1958-60 sunburst Standard. Instead the company chose to market a gold-top variant with single-coil pickups and a black Custom with two large humbuckers. Nonetheless, both models fared very well in their first year and by 1969 their combined sales topped 5000 units, enough to represent almost 20 per cent of the production of Gibson electrics. The gold-top, ineptly called the Les Paul Standard, was upgraded to Deluxe status after receiving mini-humbuckers formerly associated with electrics from

Gibson's second brand, Epiphone (and also the Gibson Firebirds). With Epi production being relocated in Japan, the cost-conscious US factory had found themselves with a surplus inventory of pickups to use up – hence the arrival of the Deluxe.

The instant success of the reissues encouraged Gibson to expand the Les Paul line with new Personal, Professional, Jumbo and Bass models that featured the low-impedance electronics long favoured by Les Paul himself on his own instruments. Thanks to the return of Les Paul guitars, and more generally the renewed popularity of solidbodies, the sales of Gibson electrics would soon regain the upper hand over acoustics. Looking back, though, the biggest electric seller during the 1961-1969 period was the one-pickup Melody Maker, albeit with a rather paltry 23,390 shipments when compared to the 47,115 LG-0s which ruled on the acoustic side. It is also interesting to note that between 1961 and 1969 a late-1950s design like the ES-335 (20,108 units) neatly outperformed the SG Standard (14,556 units) or even the cheaper SG Junior (18,059 units).

Meanwhile, to commemorate Gibson's 75th anniversary in 1969, Stan Rendell used the finest woods he had procured for the Citation. Based on the Johnny Smith model, it was meant as a superlative flagship of Gibson craftsmanship – with a resounding price of $2,500 at a time when a Super 400CESN fetched a mere $1,360. As it turned out, the exclusive Citation helped celebrate a change of ownership as Gibson's parent, CMI, was taken over in 1969 by a concern unknown to the music industry called Ecuadorian Company Limited. ECL was subsequently renamed Norlin, and gradually took Gibson through a long and pathetic decline that would last until the mid 1980s. At Gibson, the end of the 1960s also marked the end of an era. ■ ANDRE DUCHOSSOIR

THE MUNSTERS and The Man From UNCLE debut on TV. The Transylvanian family (Lily, age 137, above left) has a simple motto: "Every cloud has a dark lining." Transcending the cold war, the United Network Command for Law and Enforcement agents Napoleon Solo (American) and Ilya Kuryakin (Russian) report to Mr Waverly (British), chiefly by talking into their pens.

PRESIDENT Johnson signs the Civil Rights Act, "ending" US racial discrimination. Three civil rights leaders who had gone missing in Mississippi are found murdered.

1965

FENDER set the pace with its colourful and stylish promotion materials, such as this 1966-67 catalogue cover (right) with artwork by Bob Perine. More unusual is the 1962 ad (far right) that, viewed today, provides an ironic premonition of the oriental domination of the industry that was to come.

ギターの名手は
フェンダーびいき
フェンダーは世界の
ギターです。

'TRANSLATION: "THE WORLD'S MOST TALENTED GUITARISTS PREFER FENDER."

THE FENDER STORY

For Fender, as for the American guitar industry as a whole, the 1960s proved the old axiom, "Be careful what you wish for; you might get it." Fender entered the new decade as one of the great American success stories, their electric solidbody guitars established as the voice of a new generation of musicians whose rock'n'roll music would dominate the 1960s and beyond.

Just as Fender's phenomenal growth through the 1950s had been impossible to imagine, so the company's continued growth through the 1960s brought problems that had been unimaginable at the beginning of the decade. By the end of the 1960s Fender would be an entirely different company. Bigger, but not better: a victim of its own success. The 1960s started off as if they would be the Fender Decade, with the sound of Fender Telecasters, Stratocasters and Jazzmasters dominating the airwaves thanks to pop, surf and country groups such as The Ventures, The Beach Boys and Buck Owens & The Buckaroos. But in spite of Fender's success, Don Randall, a 50/50 partner with Leo Fender in Fender Sales, had never felt secure. Historically, new musical fads – rock'n'roll being a prime example – had sent once-popular instruments such as the classic (five-string) banjo, mandolin, tenor banjo, acoustic guitar and electric archtop guitar into near obscurity. Randall was understandably fearful that the electric solidbody guitar – essentially Fender's only product – was heading for the same fate in the 1960s. "You're always wondering if the public's fickleness is going to change musical taste," he says. "The electric organ came and went, and our electric piano [the mid-1960s Fender Rhodes] created quite a stir at one time, then faded out of the picture. The funniest was when distortion came in [during the late 1960s]. We were beating our brains out trying to make a clean amplifier, and the fellas were wanting something that would distort."

The historical pattern was broken in the 1960s, however, when the guitar wave became a juggernaut, broadening into different styles of guitar music. To further break historical patterns, guitarists of the new folk music boom were not grabbing the newest, most technologically advanced guitar to create their music. Now, the next big new thing was an old thing – the acoustic flat-top guitar. For Fender's major competitors, all of whom made flat-top guitars, the folk boom was a gift

△ FENDER MARAUDER
Prototypes only 1965-1966; this example December 1966

The rarest Fender of all: the model that never made it into production. Marauder prototypes from 1965, as glimpsed in Fender's 1965-66 catalogue (opposite), show the model with an apparent lack of pickups, although they are "hidden" below the pickguard. Later test versions, such as the one shown here, have a peculiar mix of multiple controls, angled frets and (at least) conventional pickups. None ever saw the inside of a music store.

GOYA imported guitars to the US from Sweden (Hagström), Japan (Greco) and Italy (Eko).

▷ GOYA RANGEMASTER 116
Produced 1965-1969; this example c1968

Goya was a brandname used at various times by a New York importing firm, and as was so often the case with distribution companies one brandname turns up on guitars from a number of different sources. This Rangemaster model, for example, is of Italian origin, reflecting a 1960s predilection for multiple control layouts, and most likely comes from the Eko factory. The vibrato, however, was provided by another Goya supplier, the Hagström company of Sweden (see also page 37).

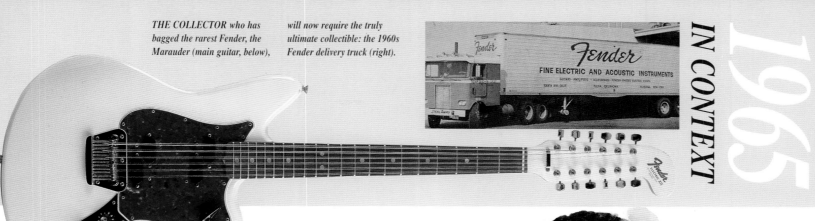

THE COLLECTOR *who has bagged the rarest Fender, the Marauder (main guitar, below),* *will now require the truly ultimate collectible: the 1960s Fender delivery truck (right).*

FENDER ELECTRIC XII
Produced 1965-1968; this example 1966

Fender reacted to the fashion for electric 12-strings created by Rickenbacker with this shortlived model, one of the first to appear after the takeover of Fender by CBS in early 1965.

from heaven. For Fender it was a potential death knell. But Don Randall was ready. First, he began distributing inexpensive imported acoustics made under the Regal brand, and in 1962 hired German-born designer Roger Rossmeisl (ex-Rickenbacker) to develop a line of Fender acoustic flat-tops, which debuted at the US trade show in 1963. But they never accounted for a significant portion of Fender sales.

In 1962 Fender introduced the Jaguar, its first new guitar since the Jazzmaster of 1958. The Jaguar was an extension of the earlier instrument, built on the Jazzmaster's 'offset waist' body shape, but with a shorter, 24" scale (Fender's standard scale length was 25.5"). It had the Jazzmaster's 'floating' vibrato and the added feature of a string-mute contained in a removable bridge cover, which most players did remove. While the short scale might seem to indicate that the Jaguar was

designed for younger players, Randall says there was a movement among professionals – the jazz players for whom the Jazzmaster had been designed but who had never adopted it – toward short-scale guitars. The Jaguar's sophisticated control system, with six switches (including on-off switches for each pickup) and two control knobs, supports Randall's contention that it was aimed at pro players.

Two years later the Mustang guitar debuted, with two pickups, a new-style vibrato and a 24" scale (with a 'three-quarter' scale length of 22" as an option). It came in red, white or blue, making it the first Fender that did not have sunburst or the benign 'blond' as standard finish. Its target market was student or teen players, clear from its $189.50 list price, just above the other budget Fenders, the short-scale Musicmaster and Duo-Sonic models.

By the mid 1960s Don Randall was feeling comfortable for the first time. But Leo Fender was not. A chronic strep infection made him wonder how much longer he had to live. And new solid-state technology made him wonder how long his self-taught knowledge of electronics would be relevant. He decided to sell. The CBS entertainment conglomerate stepped forward with an offer of $13 million, and the deal was closed

LEO FENDER (above) set up his company in the late 1940s, and sold out to CBS in 1965.

FENDER's publicity department made a rare gaffe in this 1965-66 catalogue (below), including a couple of Marauder prototypes that never actually went into production.

△ GUYATONE LG-200T
Produced 1965-1969; this example c1966

The Japanese version of the multi-control/multi-pickup idea reached a zenith with this model, generally considered as the Guyatone company's finest electric guitar of the 1960s. It has 24 frets, stereo circuitry (note the twin output jacks), and a potentially large variety of sounds from its four pickups and six associated selector switches. The well-established Guyatone company, based in Tokyo, had begun to make electric guitars during the late 1950s – but for more on its 1960s activities see the Japanese section on pages 64-69.

US MARINES *and Australian troops arrive in South Vietnam. American planes bomb North Vietnam targets in the first US retaliatory raids. President Johnson says he will continue "actions that are justified as necessary for the defence of South Vietnam". In June, US troops go on their first Vietcong offensive; by July there are 125,000 US troops in Vietnam.*

THE SOUND OF MUSIC *is released, achieving irritatingly widespread popularity. One reviewer thoughtfully warns moviegoers who are "allergic to singing nuns and sweetly innocent children".*

RUSSIAN *cosmonaut Alexei Leonov is the first man to "walk" in space, leaving his Voskhod II craft for 10 minutes during its 26-hour flight.*

SPIKE JONES, *founder of outrageously mad City Slickers group, dies in Los Angeles. Saul Hudson is born in England. In the 1980s he will become Slash, guitarist of outrageously riotous Guns N'Roses group.*

CARNABY STREET *is the centre of Swinging London, selling op-art mini dresses, PVC "kinky" boots, coloured tights and soft bras, as modelled by Jean Shrimpton and Twiggy.*

A SPEED LIMIT *of 70mph is imposed on UK motorways. Scottish driver Jim Clark is the World Grand Prix champion for the second time.*

1965

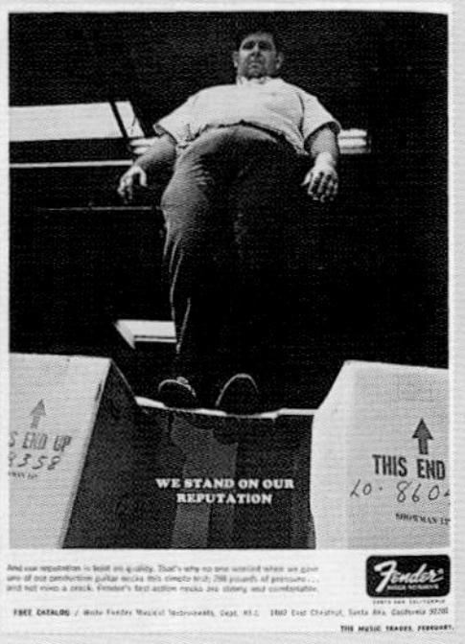

CBS bought Fender in January 1965, poured in a great deal of money, and changed many of the existing working practices. Gradually, quality suffered and reports of sloppy workmanship filtered back to HQ from the disgruntled sales force. This alarming 1967 ad (left) was part of the PR job designed to reassure dealers that Fenders were as well-made as ever.

on January 5th 1965. A pre-sale report to CBS advised that Leo was not essential, that a competent manufacturing executive and a competent chief engineer could do a better job. So Leo was contracted, but seldom-used, as a consultant for five years. Don Randall was considered essential, and he was made vice president and general manager of Fender and later president of CBS's musical instrument division.

The future looked rosy at first. Randall didn't have Leo, but he had all the resources of CBS Labs. And popular music played right into his hands. The arrival of The Beatles in America in 1964 ensured that the guitar was here to stay. And in 1965 The Byrds, an electric guitar band, hit with 'Mr Tambourine Man', a song written by the leading folk voice, Bob Dylan. With that single blow, the acoustic/electric dividing line between folk and rock music was obliterated.

With the same line-expansion philosophy that had spawned the acoustic flat tops, Fender once again called on Roger Rossmeisl, this time to develop a line of semi-hollow archtops to compete with Gibson's highly successful ES-335. Fender unveiled Rossmeisl's thin-bodied, double-cutaway Coronado line in January 1966. With Wildwood colours available, the Coronados looked good, and with the traditional Fender neck, they felt good, but they didn't sound good. Many felt that Fender simply wasn't an archtop guitar company or, for that

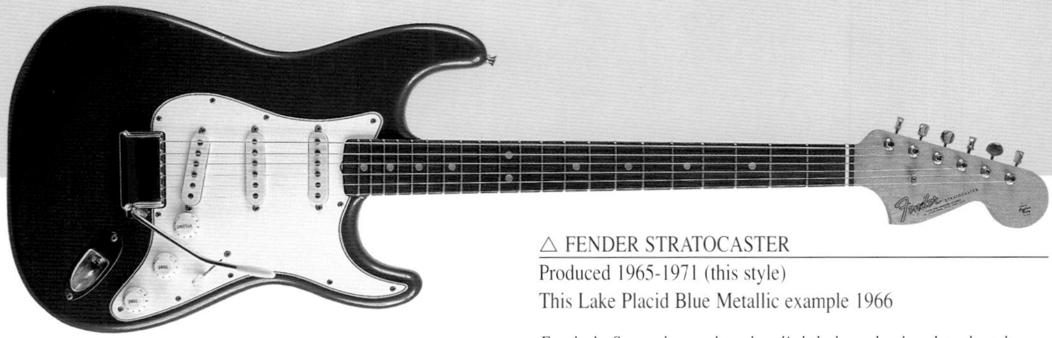

△ FENDER STRATOCASTER
Produced 1965-1971 (this style)
This Lake Placid Blue Metallic example 1966

Fender's Strat changed to the slightly broader headstock style seen here during 1965, intended to ease warping problems of the earlier, narrower design (as on the 1964 example below).

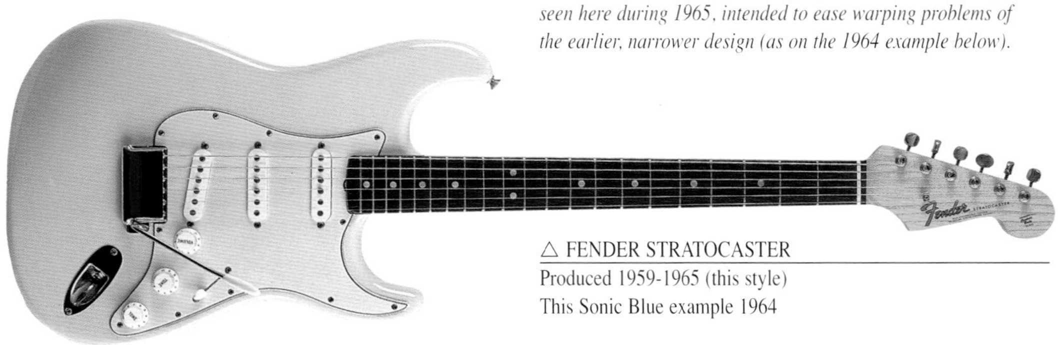

△ FENDER STRATOCASTER
Produced 1959-1965 (this style)
This Sonic Blue example 1964

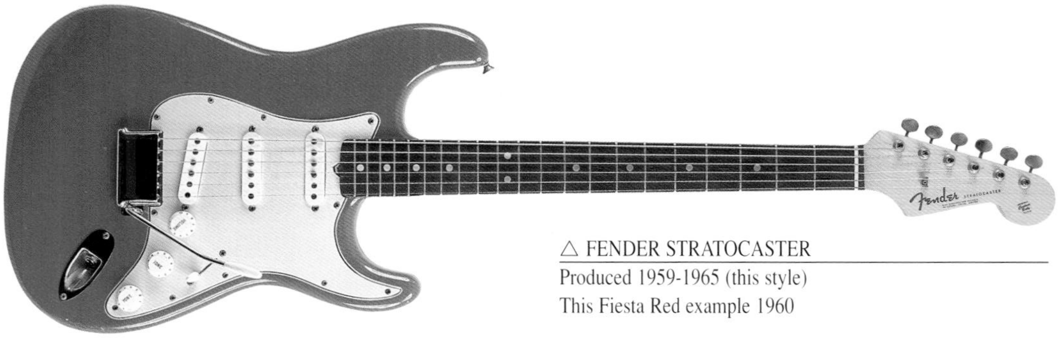

△ FENDER STRATOCASTER
Produced 1959-1965 (this style)
This Fiesta Red example 1960

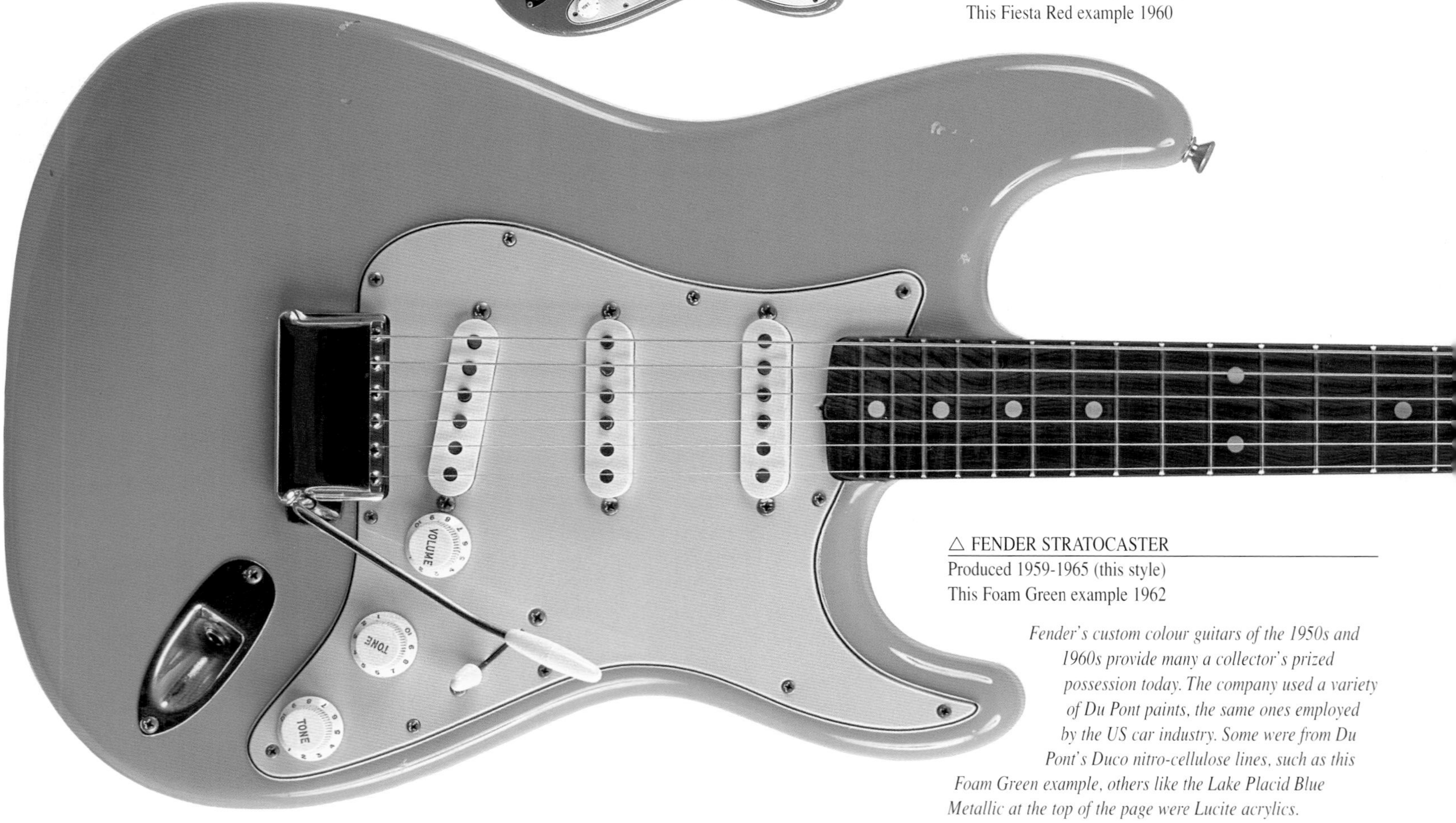

△ FENDER STRATOCASTER
Produced 1959-1965 (this style)
This Foam Green example 1962

Fender's custom colour guitars of the 1950s and 1960s provide many a collector's prized possession today. The company used a variety of Du Pont paints, the same ones employed by the US car industry. Some were from Du Pont's Duco nitro-cellulose lines, such as this Foam Green example, others like the Lake Placid Blue Metallic at the top of the page were Lucite acrylics.

matter, an acoustic guitar company. "It was an attempt to broaden the line, but it didn't broaden," says Bill Carson, production manager at the time, of the flat-top and archtop lines. "We weren't geared for it. We didn't know how to make those things." Rossmeisl's final designs for Fender came in 1969 with a pair of full-depth archtops, the Montego and LTD, which were more respected but much less successful even than the Coronados.

In the solidbody line, Fender made no lasting advances. There was the Electric XII 12-string in 1965 and the new Bronco student model in 1968. Fender sought to bolster sales of the Telecaster by 'fixing' its weight problem in 1968 with the Thinline Telecaster — which was not thinner but hollowed out on one side to reduce weight. The hollow area was signified by the addition of an f-hole on the bass side of the body. The Thinline Telecaster would be revamped with a pair

of humbucking pickups in the early 1970s, but it never amounted to more than a footnote in Telecaster history. At the end of the 1960s two more Telecaster variations appeared — the shortlived Paisley Red and Blue Flower psychedelics, and the Rosewood model — that are more noteworthy for their collectability now than for their impact at the time.

The least noteworthy Fenders of the 1960s, but the most indicative of CBS's influence, are two obscure models from 1969 that had a total of five names: the Musiclander/ Swinger/Arrow and the Custom/Maverick. These were 'parts' guitars, put together and adapted from various leftover materials and work-in-progress of other models.

Fender's stumbling in the guitar market was symptomatic of a bureaucratic disease that was weakening the company from the inside. "CBS didn't hurt the company initially," Randall says. "It was after they had the company three or four years that they did damage to it. We had systems analysts running out of our ears, engineers running out of our ears that weren't envisioned when the sale was made and were totally unnecessary. We had to document everything we used and make where-used files for every nut, bolt and screw, and make a drawing for it."

CBS's ignorance of electric guitars began to show, and Don Randall's attention had been diverted by

corporate duties. "I was the only division president outside of New York," he says. "When they had a meeting in New York I had to jump on a red-eye special. Like most meetings they were non-productive." Increasingly frustrated, Randall resigned in 1969.

CBS had pumped plenty of money into Fender — starting with a $2.7 million, 120,000-square-foot building in 1966 — and the investment appeared to be paying off. Sales climbed "almost geometrically", Randall says. And the manufacturing staff practically doubled, from around 500 in 1964 to 950 in 1969. But the company was becoming an empty shell.

As the 1960s ended, Fender was no longer leading the guitar boom, only riding the momentum of its earlier success. When the boom ended with the recession of the early 1970s, followed by the keyboard insurrection (that Don Randall had feared), Fender would have no inner strength to pull it through. With no Leo Fender, no Don Randall, only faceless corporate management, Fender ended the 1960s, its most successful decade, set up for a long, painful decline through the 1970s. ■ WALTER CARTER

△ FENDER STRATOCASTER
Produced 1965-1971 (this style)
This Black example October 1966

Session musician Al Kooper owned this Strat, which he says was given to him by Jimi Hendrix when Kooper worked on the Electric Ladyland album in New York in 1968. Hendrix used a variety of Strats, including black models, during the 1960s.

▽ FENDER STRATOCASTER
Produced 1959-1965 (this style)
This Burgundy Mist Metallic example 1961

JIMI HENDRIX (above) was, as one Fender executive put it, "responsible for more Strats being sold than all the Fender salesmen put together". At the start of his career Hendrix used a tatty sunburst Strat, but soon began to acquire more, usually opting for a black or white model on-stage. He preferred maple-fingerboard models (above) from mid-1968.

1966

JEFF BECK was one of the most inventive and intuitive guitarists of the 1960s. As a Yardbird, Beck drew all kinds of new sounds from his Fender, even turning it into a sitar with a fuzzbox for 'Heart Full of Soul' (1965), while later he encouraged new demand for old Les Pauls. In the Jeff Beck Group he turned in some fine performances, such as the fluid instrumental 'Beck's Bolero'.

ROCK & POP GUITARS

As above, so below. Chaos theory tells us that little things reflect big ones. Or, to be more precise, that all things great and small share the same basic characteristics, and the differences are purely those of scale. If the definitive Sound Of The Sixties was the sound of rock guitar, then the reasons are simple and straightforward: the 1960s were a decade of turbulence, of change, of restlessness and hunger and boundless curiosities and a sense of infinite possibilities.

It was a decade for the creation of new ideas, and for redefining and recombining old ones – and this holds equally true for the massive shifts in the social and political spheres as it does for the comparatively smaller one of games people played with wood, wires and valves. The sound of the 1960s was the sound of barriers breaking down, of systems going into overload, distortion and – ultimately – feedback.

The guitar was the iconic signifier of the rock of the 1950s, but on record it had to jostle some heavy competition for the audio spotlight. For every totemic six-stringer like Chuck Berry, Buddy Holly or Eddie Cochran, there was an equally charismatic pianist like Little Richard, Jerry Lee Lewis or Fats Domino. It's true that in much of the classic pop of the 1960s – the cinerama-scaled epics of Phil Spector, Bacharach & David and the Tamla-Motown combine, or the funky dancefloor epiphanies of James Brown and Stax Records, where Jimmy Nolen and Steve Cropper cut through the orchestration with their six-string razors – the guitarist remained strictly part of the ensemble. Nevertheless, at the rockier end of white pop

music the guitar moved closer and closer to stage-centre until, by mid-decade, the 'guitar hero' had emerged as a fully-fledged phenomenon.

In the United States, guitar-driven instrumental singles by the likes of Dick Dale and The Ventures were an indispensable accessory to the surf music phenomenon, but The Ventures' UK counterparts, The Shadows, maintained a dual role as backing group to boy-next-door pop idol Cliff Richard, and therefore were far more closely allied to the pop mainstream.

The Beatles arrived at the tail end of 1962, revolutionising pop with their uniquely innovative blend of Motown and rockabilly and sending guitar and amplifier sales through the ceiling. They, and the first wave of 'beat group' successes following in their immediate wake, focused squarely on The Singers & The Song, their guitarists specialising in clean, tight ensemble playing with texture and rhythm prioritised over improvisation or extravagant soloing. John Lennon's rhythms were chunky and driving, Paul McCartney's bass pumping and melodic, George Harrison's leads crisp, composed and rehearsed down to the tiniest inflection. Within months The Beatles' hegemony was challenged by The Rolling Stones whose studiedly sullen bohemianism and deep roots in Chicago blues made them a very different proposition to the cheery Scousers. They did, however, share The Beatles' ensemble guitar ethic, albeit in a manner derived from the Muddy Waters combos of the 1950s. Keith Richards and Brian Jones welded their instruments together so closely and intuitively that in much of their material the distinction between 'lead' and 'rhythm' guitars

almost disappeared. Keith specialised in the Chuck Berry stuff (both signature ringin'-a-bell riffs and runka-runka rhythms) and Brian handled the slide-slinging, but almost everything else, guitar-wise, was up for grabs.

The modern guitar era – with its emphasis on cranked-up power chording, complex riffing, science-fiction sound processing and extended soloing – can trace itself back to three bands which emerged in the R&B

JIMI HENDRIX was of course best known for playing a Strat, but during the last half of 1967 this black Flying V was his favourite guitar. The extra decorations were painted by Jimi; he also converted the nut for left- or right-hand stringing.

THE MONKEES were given Gretsch gear (right) for their 1966 TV series. Session guitarists on their records included Glen Campbell, James Burton, Sonny Curtis and Jerry McGee (who probably played the driving arpeggios of 'Last Train To Clarksville').

▽ GRETSCH MONKEES
Produced 1966-1967; this example 1967

TV company Screen Gems offered Gretsch the option to sell a Monkees-related instrument. This model, emblazoned with the Monkees guitar-shaped logo, was the shortlived result.

DICK DALE (right) had a hit in 1961, 'Let's Go Trippin', that defined the sound of the surf instrumental. Left-hander Dale poured out surging, staccato Strat lines, borrowed scales from his east-European heritage, and set it all adrift in a sea of reverb. Fans said the powerful result was the aural equivalent of catching a wave, and Dale was dubbed the "king

of the surf guitar". There were cash-in movies (Muscle Beach Party, far right; Dale is at the back with a youthful Stevie Wonder) and hits for other bands, including The Surfaris' 'Wipe Out', The Chantays' 'Pipeline' and The Beach Boys' 'Surfin USA'. Guitar makers (like Kent, above) exploited the upsurge in demand, but surf didn't last much beyond the British invasion of 1964.

slipstream of the Stones, though each of them swiftly distanced themselves from the blues. The Kinks and The Who distinguished themselves from R&B's huddled masses by thunderous all-action stage shows, radio-canny songcraft (provided respectively by Ray Davies and Pete Townshend) and the kind of murderously crunchy wall-of-sound guitar abuse (courtesy of Ray's kid brother Dave and, again, Townshend) which turned the Power Chord and the Killer Riff into contemporary guitar grails.

However, the real signpost to the future was provided by The Yardbirds, the first band whose key player was the guitarist rather than the singer. Their vocalist, the late Keith Relf, had the consistent misfortune to be effortlessly upstaged, first by Eric Clapton, then by Clapton's successor Jeff Beck, and finally by Jimmy Page . who, in the latter part of

the decade, presided over the demise of the group and its eventual resurrection as the 1970s-dominating Led Zeppelin.

Clapton may not have been rock's first virtuoso guitarist, but he was the first to be perceived as such by fans rather than fellow musicians. 'Musicianship' had never before been an essential criterion for assessing rock groups. It had always been more important to have good songs, an exciting stage act, pretty faces and cool clothes than to include a guitarist or drummer capable of impressing jazz critics. The revelation that changed the game was Clapton's wholesale importation into rock of the 1950s and 1960s innovations of urban blues maestri like BB King, Albert King, Freddy King, Otis Rush and Buddy Guy: thick, overdriven tone, singing sustain and fleet-fingered, impassioned solo marathons, all packaged with a tight-lipped, introverted, artist-at-work persona. Clapton truly came into his own when he quit The Yardbirds on the brink of their first pop success to dive headlong into the muddy waters of straight-no-chaser blues purism with John Mayall's Bluesbreakers. In that band he once again

◁ GIBSON FLYING V

Produced 1966-1970 (this style); this example circa March 1967

Jimi Hendrix used this Flying V constantly in 1967. Hendrix later gave the guitar to Eire Apparent guitarist Mick Cox, since when it has been through a variety of owners, most of whom were unaware of its pedigree. The V's present owner, musician David Brewis, bought it in 1995 and restored the original black paintwork as well as Jimi's wild psychedelic additions. At first Brewis was unsure if the V belonged to Hendrix, but authenticity was confirmed when the unique patterns in its plastic fingerboard dots were found to match exactly those on a detailed period photograph of the guitar.

ONLY 44 of Gibson's reissued Flying Vs made in 1967 were not in the standard cherry finish. Hendrix's V would have been one of the few black guitars among those 44.

THE VOX FACTORY in England in 1965 (below). Some necks and whole guitars were also made in Italy. Vox began a reciprocal distribution deal with the American Thomas Organ Co in 1964. Soon Thomas had extra US-made Vox amps, but by 1969 the original British Vox operation would be closed.

THE HOLLIES were among the most professional British beat groups of the 1960s. They displayed good playing and fine harmony vocals amid some of the best pop songs of the time. Guitarist Tony Hicks (right) added crisp, concise solos to the singles, sometimes using a Vox

Phantom XII 12-string (right) as well as his Gibson ES-345 and Les Paul Junior. The group's albums developed from singles-plus-a-few to strong collections, with their fine Evolution LP (above) having the misfortune to appear the same month as Sgt Pepper.

ALL-VOX MAN . . . that's TONY HICKS

▽ VOX GUITAR ORGAN
Produced 1966-67; this example c1966

Guitar makers have never quite managed to convince players that a guitar which can sound like a keyboard is a good idea. Vox pioneered the guitar organ, but trying effectively to put the sound generators of their Continental organ into a Phantom guitar proved highly unreliable. The fraught project was shortlived, and few fully-working models survive.

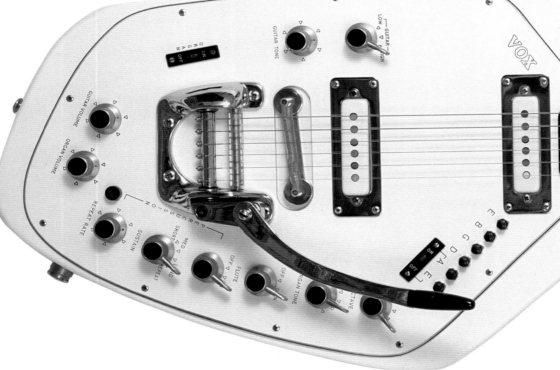

THE VOX Guitar Organ had an array of keyboard effects (left). Frets were wired to tone generators in the body; a string touching a fret completed a circuit and produced a note.

WILDWOOD was a special finish achieved by injecting coloured dyes into beech. It was available on some Coronado models, in various colour combinations (see ad, right).

A Grand NEW Guitar from Fender The Antigua

FENDER offered some Coronados in its shaded white-to-brown Antigua finish.

△ FENDER CORONADO XII WILDWOOD II
Coronado XII produced 1966-1969; this example 1968

Fender were kings when it came to solidbody electrics, but lost out to the increasing popularity of hollow-body electrics during the 1960s. So the Coronados were introduced to compete with Gretsches and Gibsons of the period, but the line proved unsuccessful and had disappeared from Fender's list by 1971.

TEISCO were not only influenced by Fender's guitars, but as this 1966 Teisco Del Rey catalogue shows (left) the style of the Californian company's promo material also caught the eye of the Japanese. Compare this luridly illustrated piece of work to the typical Fender example shown on page 40.

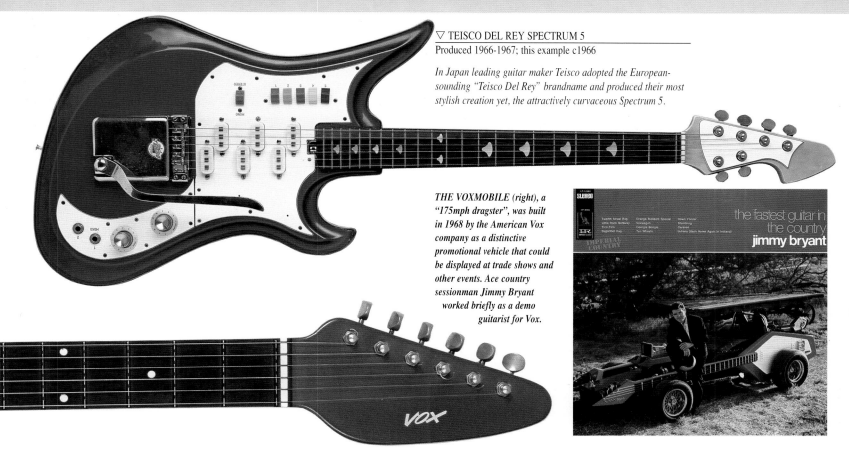

▽ TEISCO DEL REY SPECTRUM 5
Produced 1966-1967; this example c1966

In Japan leading guitar maker Teisco adopted the European-sounding "Teisco Del Rey" brandname and produced their most stylish creation yet, the attractively curvaceous Spectrum 5.

THE VOXMOBILE (right), a "175mph dragster", was built in 1968 by the American Vox company as a distinctive promotional vehicle that could be displayed at trade shows and other events. Ace country sessionman Jimmy Bryant worked briefly as a demo guitarist for Vox.

remorselessly outshone the frontman and became the primary drawing card. If Clapton was blues-rock guitar's brooding Hamlet, Jeff Beck was its cackling, demonic Joker. With little more than a slide, an echo unit and a fuzz-box as props, he delighted in peeling off ear-teasing speed-runs and aurally disguising himself as violin, sitar, train-whistle, chicken-coop or car-wreck. Enthusiastically pillaging and pastiching Indian raga, Gregorian chant and all manner of esoteric exotica, The Yardbirds eagerly embraced the omnivorous eclecticism that became a hallmark of 'progressive' guitar-based 1960s rock.

Reeling under the onslaught of the British Invasion, the empire struck back with folk-rock. Swathed in immaculately executed vocal harmonies and bristling with fingerpicked electric 12-strings, American folk-rock was essentially the creation of The Byrds. The group's leader and mastermind Jim McGuinn (later Roger – don't ask, it's a 1960s thang) wedded Beatlesque instrumentation to Dylanoid singer-songwriting via his own wavery voice and jingle-jangle Rickenbacker. Dylan's electric recordings actually placed more emphasis on layers of keyboards and The Zim's own tootling mouth-harp than it did on guitars, despite the studio presence of Mike Bloomfield whose flashy, hyperthyroid work with Chicago's defiantly unpop Paul Butterfield Blues Band had made him America's closest equivalent to Eric Clapton.

Folk-rock of a different, less shinily-packaged variety was the basis for American guitar's next major move, though LSD,

revamped 1950s beatnikism and the sudden availability of extremely powerful amplifiers were also key factors. The first wave of San Francisco 'hippie' bands essentially consisted of very loud folk groups on psychedelic drugs. The early guitar sounds of Jefferson Airplane (Jorma Kaukonen), Grateful Dead (Jerry Garcia, Bob Weir), Big Brother & The Holding Company (Sam Andrew, James Gurley) and Country Joe & The Fish (Barry Melton) seemed an uneasy meld of folk-club fingerpicking and megawatt fuzz-boxed bluesrocking performed by players who sounded like they'd only recently dumped their banjos and Martins for 335s and Marshalls.

Easily the finest and most resourceful electric guitarist to emerge from the San Francisco scene was The Grateful Dead's Jerry Garcia. Indeed, the Dead turned out to be that scene's most durable and consistent band, though they were far from a one-man show. Their high card was the synergy between the band's four core members, but Garcia's sparkling, phoenix-like guitar sparked their idiosyncratic blend of free-form improvisation and roots-music authenticity. Both Garcia as an individual and the Dead as a collective had one foot planted in folk and country, the other in blues and soul... and the head somewhere in both inner and outer space.

Brits and Yanks compared notes, famously, at the 1967 Monterey International Pop Festival. The West Coasters were a peacefully stoned bunch mostly off their faces on both Californian sunshine and California Sunshine. If they were shattered by the volume and violence of The Who they were

absolutely vaporised by Jimi Hendrix. Sounding like a Starship Enterprise co-piloted by Curtis Mayfield and John Coltrane crash landing at maximum warp on the south side of Chicago, and looking like an extremely chilled-out Brazilian buccaneer who'd just looted Carnaby Street, Hendrix rewrote the sacred texts of the electric guitar more profoundly than any other single individual, before or since.

Drawing freely on avant-garde jazz, down-home blues, grits-and-groceries funk and the brave new rock world unveiled by Bob Dylan and The Beatles, Hendrix demonstrated – more dramatically than anybody could possibly have imagined – just how broad a canvas was now at a rock guitarist's disposal, and how bright and varied a palette of colours could be applied to it.

Jimi Hendrix was to the electric guitar what Bruce Lee was to the martial arts. Famously, the Little Dragon once told a questioner who enquired what style he fought in, "My style is no style." What he meant was that he was tied to no single discipline, but drew what he needed from whatever he found, wherever he found it. Hendrix was by no means the only guitarist of his era who could play in a variety of different styles, but none of his contemporaries was capable of matching him for the sheer vision with which he melded seemingly disparate influences into a single, coherent music. He had it all covered. He could play straight, deep blues with greater emotional and idiomatic authenticity than Eric Clapton, top Jeff Beck's mastery of electronic and technique-freak special effects, and trump Pete Townshend at both on-stage showmanship and power-chord monumentalism. Hendrix's fusion of 'black' and 'white'

1967

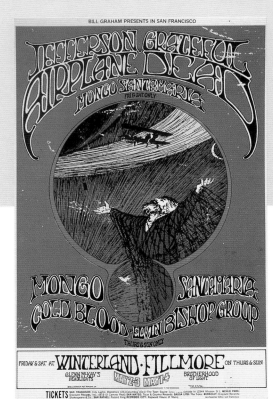

MOBY GRAPE (with lead guitarist Jerry Miller), The Grateful Dead (Jerry Garcia, Bob Weir) and Jefferson Airplane (Jorma Kaukonen) were at the centre of the stoned San Francisco sound. The extended, tripped-out solos that these West Coast psychedelic bands pioneered took the guitar to its most inspired heights... and to its most tedious lengths.

and 'English' and 'American' idioms and elements also combined the advanced production techniques pioneered by The Beatles with allusive, poetic lyrics derived from Bob Dylan. In a decade obsessed with opening up and exploring hitherto uncharted areas of possibility, Hendrix was as important symbolically as musically, as iconic a figure as Dylan or The Beatles. Certainly for guitarists, he was a 100-watt revelation on legs.

Thus inspired, rock guitar was busy gobbling up every arcane influence it could find. In LA, The Doors' Robbie Krieger was enthusiastically transplanting techniques to his solidbody Gibson that he'd acquired as a student of flamenco stylings. In

Manhattan, Lou Reed super-charged his garage-band basics with avant-garde drones derived, via his Velvet Underground colleague John Cale, from contemporary minimalist composer LaMonte Young. The result was something so far ahead of its time that many had trouble recognising it as music at all until the Velvets were long disbanded. And back in England Pink Floyd's Syd Barrett was exploiting the electric guitar's potential for pure sound, while Richard Thompson and Fairport Convention laid the groundwork for a distinctively British folk-rock idiom by electrifying and psychedlicising Anglo-Celtic musical traditions.

ERIC CLAPTON's SG (below) started life with a Maestro vibrato unit, but this was not to the guitarist's taste. After a number of changes, the guitar currently has a non-original bridge and tailpiece. It has also had a new headstock fitted, part of the neck has been replaced, the knobs have been changed and the paintwork carefully retouched.

△ GIBSON SG STANDARD
Painted 1967 (SG Standard introduced 1963)

This is Eric Clapton's famous psychedelic SG. He bought the guitar probably in early 1967 to replace his stolen Les Paul Standard. Soon Clapton had a Dutch group of artists known as The Fool paint the guitar. They set a fiery-haired angel amid stars and clouds, added an idyllic landscape to the pickguard, and put an explosively 1960s version of a sunburst finish on the back (below). Clapton used the guitar widely with Cream, both on-stage and for recordings such as the Disraeli Gears and Wheels Of Fire albums. Since 1974 the guitar has been owned by musician/producer Todd Rundgren.

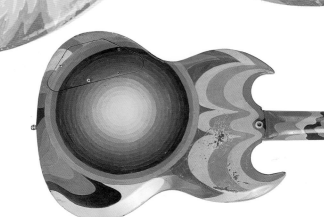

THE GRATEFUL DEAD underlined the musical superiority of the West Coast bands with the visual style of their LP sleeves (Aoxomoxoa, right). But one of the earliest psychedelic groups came from Texas. The 13th Floor Elevators used overt op-art for the cover of their 1966 album, a record which was full of Roky Erickson's blazing guitar.

JERRY GARCIA (above) defined the freewheeling improvisational spirit at the heart of The Grateful Dead, along with guitarist Bob Weir and bassist Phil Lesh.

A vogue for jazz-rock, spearheaded by Blood Sweat & Tears and Chicago, meant bolting horn sections onto rock rhythm sections, with loud, fuzzboxed, feedbacked guitar an essential ingredient. Rock-raised guitarists had little aptitude for the harmonic complexities of jazz, and younger jazz guitarists like Larry Coryell who fancied growing their hair and plugging into Marshall stacks experienced equally severe problems handling the technology that was second nature to their rocking cousins. Just about the only guys comfortable on both sides of the fence were John McLaughlin, who formed his Mahavishnu Orchestra at the tail end of the decade, and Carlos Santana, essentially a blues guitarist fronting a percussion-heavy Latin combo.

Then there were those who reacted to the preponderance of deafening, fussily over-arranged 'progressive' rock by working on their vocal harmonies and blowing the dust off their acoustics, or by crossing the cultural and ideological barriers separating long-haired, anti-war, free-loving, pot-smoking rock from patriotic, rural, God-fearing country music. The Byrds' album *Sweetheart Of The Rodeo* and the austere acousticisms of a revitalised Bob Dylan commenced a vogue for laidback, plangent, extremely white 'mellow' music which would reach its apogee in the 1970s.

Rock ended the 1960s altered beyond recognition. A once monolithic form had splintered into a series of hyphenates: folk-rock, jazz-rock, blues-rock, country-rock, and the all-encompassing 'progressive rock'. But looming above all else was the Godzilla of heavy metal: gigawatt riff-rock exemplified on the one hand by Led Zeppelin's paradoxical blend of sophisticated eclecticism and phallocentric vulgarity, and on the other by the barbiturate lumbering of Britain's Black Sabbath or America's Grand Funk Railroad. By the time their long and winding road took them to *Abbey Road*, even The Beatles were cautiously giving heavy a go. But on Planet Metal itself, singers had become almost incidental, and rock guitar had become an Olympic event wherein players were scored for strength, speed and volume. Something had to give, and in the 1970s and 1980s it did. But, for better and/or for worse, it was during the 1960s that rock guitar became, for all intents and purposes, what it still is today. ■ CHARLES SHAAR MURRAY

THE FOOL were three Dutch artists (above, left to right): Simon Posthuma, Marijke Koger and Josje Leeger, with a Canadian, Barry Finch, added for their album. Moving to London in the 1960s, The Fool painted the exterior of the Apple boutique, as well as a car and a piano for John Lennon. They worked on Eric Clapton's SG (pictured right) in 1967.

LOTUS EUROPE

GEORGE got this famous Rickenbacker in 1964, but first tried a 12-string back in April 1963. "Tom Springfield had a big 12-string," George told Melody Maker. "I sat playing it in the dressing room all afternoon. What a sound!"

THE BEATLES' first live TV appearance in the US was The Ed Sullivan Show (below) when 70 million US viewers saw Paul on Höfner bass, George playing a Gretsch Country Gent and John on his Rickenbacker "old-style" 325. Vox exploited the group's use of their amps to gain a foothold in the US market with ads such as this (right) in the trade press.

Thousands of would-be guitarists wrestled with a chord or three as The Beatles made the electric guitar the happening sound of the 1960s. But which guitars did the Fab Four themselves play, exactly?

It is the evening of February 9th 1964, and in CBS TV's Studio 50 in Manhattan, New York, the very first shots of The British Invasion are being fired. The Beatles have been in the United States just three days, and they're into the opening bars of 'All My Loving', the first song of their debut live American TV broadcast on *The Ed Sullivan Show*.

George harmonises with John behind Paul's lead vocal,

then adjusts the volume control on his Gretsch Chet Atkins Country Gentleman, takes centre stage, and plays a short country/rockabilly-inspired solo. As he moves over to join Paul at the other mike for the second verse, a good number of the 70 million Americans who are watching imagine themselves as the grinning lead guitarist in just such a group, with just such a Gretsch around their shoulders. Or maybe they'd prefer the moody role of John the rhythm guitarist, with his black Rickenbacker 325?

George and John are playing these particular guitars because of an American country music hero and a Belgian harmonica player. George idolises Chet Atkins, the foremost country picker in Nashville. Atkins helps everyone from Elvis to

the Everly Brothers in the studio, makes great guitarists'-guitarist records of his own, and since the mid 1950s has lent a hand to the Gretsch company of New York to design a series of Chet Atkins electric guitar models. George bought his double-cutaway Gretsch Chet Atkins Country Gent in London in summer 1963, just in time to record 'She Loves You'. Three

▽ GEORGE HARRISON'S RICKENBACKER 360/12
360/12 produced 1963-current; this example December 1963

Rickenbacker gave this 12-string to George during the group's first US visit in February 1964. It provided brand new guitar sounds, not least on the opening chord of 'A Hard Day's Night'.

△ GEORGE HARRISON'S GRETSCH DUO JET
Duo Jet produced 1953-1961 (this style); this example 1957

George's first proper US-made guitar, purchased around 1961 from a sailor who brought it back to Liverpool from an American trip. "It may have been secondhand," George said later, "but I polished that thing, I was so proud to own it." He used this Duo Jet regularly through the early years of Beatle fame until he bought his Country Gentleman in London in the summer of 1963.

△ JOHN LENNON'S RICKENBACKER 325
325 produced c1963-1975; this example February 1964

On that decisive first US trip in February 1964 Rickenbacker also had the good sense to provide John with this replacement for his old-style 325 model. He immediately took to the new gift, and used the guitar you see here on all the important Beatles live dates and recordings up to the point when he bought an Epiphone Casino (see p.53) in 1966 for the Revolver sessions.

HAMBURG *provided a tough training ground for The Beatles who played five stints in the northern-German city between summer 1960 and the end of 1962. "The booze was flowing and people were having a good time," drummer Pete Best later* told Gareth Pawlowski. "The Germans really loved the Ray Charles classic 'What'd I Say' because they could participate by echoing the lyrics and banging their beer bottles on the table." This picture (above) from one of the Hamburg dives, *probably taken in 1960, shows original bassist Stuart Sutcliffe (front) playing his large-bodied Höfner bass. Behind, George plays the Neoton/Futurama guitar which provided him with workmanlike service during his first months in the group.*

51

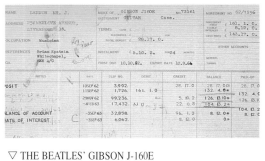

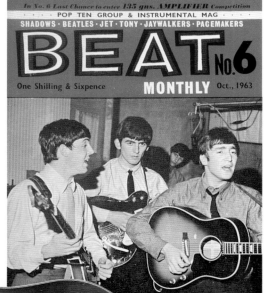

▽ THE BEATLES' GIBSON J-160E
J-160E produced 1954-1979; this example June 1962

One of the group's two "jumbo" Gibsons, which they used as normal acoustics or amplified. Owned today by George, this one was actually down originally on John's HP agreement (above).

years earlier in Hamburg, Germany, John had seen Jean 'Toots' Thielemans playing not his customary mouth organ but a Rickenbacker guitar. John fell in love with the look and the name and, on a visit to a Hamburg music store with an amp-hunting George, got himself a Rickenbacker 325. "I sold my Höfner, made a profit on it too, and bought a Rickenbacker," John told an interviewer a few years later. "It's the most beautiful guitar."

But these weren't the first electric guitars that either Beatle had used. Back in 1960 The Beatles were like any other young group starting out: they had no money to buy good instruments, and got by with anything they could scrape together – despite John's joke in a 1961 *Mersey Beat* magazine that suddenly they "all grew guitars". George moved from a Höfner President to a Höfner Club 40 hollow-body electric, and then a solidbody Neoton Grazioso (or Futurama, as it was soon renamed).

During 1960 the fledgling guitar trio – George, John and Paul – added a bass player and a drummer, and the fab five's manager rather remarkably secured them no less than 48 nights from mid-August at the Indra club in Hamburg. They took their basic guitars with them: Paul (still a guitarist) had a

JOHN and George each bought a J-160E in 1962. John is seen with his while George plays the Gretsch Country Gent on this 1963 magazine cover (above).

THE BEATLES created an enormous surge of interest in guitars and guitar playing during the 1960s. Italian guitarist and designer Mario Maccaferri (below) had moved to New York in 1939 and first made cheap plastic guitars in 1953. Sensing an opportunity with the Beatles boom, Mario's Mastro company had by summer 1964 made 500,000 plastic Beatles guitars (right) retailing at between 98¢ and $19.95. Collectors today pay rather more, especially if they have the original package.

BEATLES GUITARS
In four sizes. Each shrink-wrapped on colorful card. Complete with pick and simple song book.

BEATLE-IST GUITAR	BEATLES YEAH-YEAH GUITAR	BEATLES FOUR POP GUITAR	BEATLES JR. GUITAR
30½". 6 strings—3 colored nylon and 3 nylon-wound.	22". 6 colored nylon strings.	21". 3 colored nylon and 1 wound string.	14¼". 3 colored nylon and 1 wound string.
No. 340 CS—	No. 330 CS—	No. 320 CS—	No. 300 CS—
⅓ doz. pack—18 lbs.	1 doz. pack—14 lbs.	1 doz. pack—14 lbs.	2 doz. pack—11 lbs.

10

£19 ($30) Dutch-made Rosetti Solid 7, John took his £28 ($45) German Höfner Club 40, and George the relatively luxurious £58 ($90) Czech-built Grazioso. Certainly, none of these was a great guitar. Fortunately, the Hamburg audience didn't require much more than a noise to drink to.

When the group returned to Liverpool, George managed to save some money for a new guitar, and through a small ad in the local newspaper acquired a late 1950s Gretsch Duo Jet from a sailor who'd brought it back from the States. Already enthralled with Chet Atkins' playing, George had to have a Gretsch. OK, so it wasn't a Chet Atkins Gretsch, but it was nonetheless that rare and remarkable thing, an American instrument. "Any good American guitar looked sensational to us," George said later. "We'd only had beat-up, crummy guitars at that stage." He soon gave away his dormant Grazioso as the prize in a magazine competition.

John continued to play his Rickenbacker, and on The Beatles' first single and LP recordings, made at EMI studios in

MUSIC SHOPS in Liverpool savoured especially plentiful business in the wake of The Beatles' phenomenal success throughout the 1960s. In their early years, the group themselves tended to favour Rushworth's and Hessy's stores in the city centre. For example, guitarist Chris Huston of fellow Liverpudlian band The Undertakers recalls a visit to Hessy's in 1960 or 1961. "John and I were pretty good friends, and not too long after he came back from Hamburg with his first Rickenbacker we went into Hessy's, where he bought a Bigsby unit from salesman Jim Gretty. John had his guitar with him, and we put it on the counter, unscrewed the old vibrato – which obviously wasn't as good – and screwed on the Bigsby." In 1962 John and George bought the famous pair of specially-imported Gibson J-160Es from nearby Rushworth's (touted as "Liverpool's largest suppliers of guitars") as this photo from Mersey Beat magazine shows (far right).

THE BACK of George's Stratocaster (left) reveals rather more of the Fender's original sonic blue custom colour, although it did not escape the artful redecoration that aligns the Beatle Fender with two other famous painted guitars of the period: Jimi Hendrix's Flying V (see p.46/46) and Eric Clapton's SG (p.48/49). The label on the rear of the headstock identifies this guitar's original sale from a music shop in Kent, England.

BEBOPALULA.

GO CAT GO.

△ GEORGE HARRISON'S FENDER STRATOCASTER
Strat Produced 1954-current: this example around December 1961

Around 1967 George took some pots of dayglo paint and transformed his sonic blue Statocaster into this highly personalised home-improved psychedelic appliance. The newly daubed Strat was just about visible – in glorious black and white – on the Our World global satellite broadcast of 'All You Need Is Love' that summer, but was more colourfully displayed on the 'I Am The Walrus' sequence from the group's Christmas TV film, Magical Mystery Tour. This Strat also turned up on many Beatle studio sessions of the period (see picture opposite), alongside two new 1966 acquisitions, an Epiphone Casino and a Gibson SG Standard, and is today one of George's favourite slide guitars.

GEORGE's most famous Beatle guitars were probably his Country Gent (featured in a Gretsch promo shot, right) and his chiming Rickenbacker 12-string. But aside from these, George and his fellow Beatles inevitably acquired other electric guitars that for one reason or another turned out to be of little use. George, for example, briefly played an obscure Rickenbacker 425 in 1963, while Gretsch and Vox made him a couple of odd custom guitars. John too was given a hard-to-play 12-string version of Rickenbacker's 325, and had a fleeting dalliance with a Gretsch Nashville.

George continued to use his 12-string – described by *Melody Maker* as "the beat boys' secret weapon" – all over The Beatles' studio and live performances. At the time George compared the Rick 12 sound to that of an organ or an electric piano, understandable when you hear something like 'I Should Have Known Better'. But perhaps the guitar's most famous studio moment is on the opening chord of 'A Hard Day's Night'. "That sound," George said much later, "you just associate with those early 1960s Beatles records."

'I Feel Fine', recorded in October 1964, can be seen now as a pointer toward things to come, in that the celebrated 'feedback' intro was deliberately concocted in the studio to get a weird sound, and edited on to the start of the piece. "Don't be put off by that opening noise," Paul told *Melody Maker* shortly afterwards. "It was a laugh. John was playing his jumbo guitar as we did the final run-through before recording, and when the red light came on for the actual session he played it unintentionally. The result's a sound of feedback, and after a bit of thought we decided to leave it in. It's the biggest gimmick thing we've ever used."

Not content with revolutionising the bassline by his exceptional four-string work deep down inside The Beatles' records, Paul began to take more interest in guitar playing, and bought himself an Epiphone Casino hollow-body electric in 1964. Being left-handed, Paul restrung the right-handed

Casino to use it 'upside down'. Although he told one magazine that he'd got it for "composing", presumably to fend off the question of why the group's bassist should need an electric six-string, by early 1965 Paul had started to use the Casino in the studio. In February, while John was playing some new recordings to Chris Roberts from *Melody Maker*, he suddenly said: "Hey, listen! Hear that playing by Paul?" This was probably during playback of 'Ticket To Ride' or 'Another Girl'. "Paul's been doing quite a bit of lead guitar work this week," John explained to Roberts. "I reckon he's moving in."

Maybe as retaliation, John and George decided to buy a couple more guitars later in 1965 in time for the *Rubber Soul* sessions. Mal Evans, the group's trusty roadie, was sent out to get a couple of Fender Stratocasters, and apparently returned with an amazing find, a matching pair of Strats in Fender's pale Sonic Blue colour. Clear evidence of the Fenders can be heard as John and George's Strats triumphantly enter the solo of 'Nowhere Man' in unison, John giving way to George alone for the cheeky pinging harmonic at its close, the potentially twangy, toppy timbre of the Fender fully exploited.

Still the apparently ceaseless live dates continued and, despite the studio experimentation with other guitars, the stage instruments generally held to the traditional line-up of Gretsches and Rickenbacker 12-string for George, Rick 325 for John, and Höfner bass for Paul.

In December 1965 George lost his Gretsch Country Gent,

smashed apart when it fell from the group's car on a drive to a gig in Scotland. Frederick James wrote soon after in *The Beatles Book*: "According to a disappointed George, at least 14 lorries must have run over the guitar before the boys located all the battered bits at the side of the motorway." Although he still had his trusty Tennessean and Rick 12-string, George soon bought a Gibson ES-345 hollow-body electric as a replacement for the Gent. Into 1966, George also got a solidbody Gibson SG Standard, and he and John acquired an Epiphone Casino each to match Paul's.

They recorded *Revolver* in 1966, an astonishing piece of work that is blatantly experimental, and as far as the guitars go is chock full of crunchy, fuzzboxed Casinos and SGs, deftly tricked into playing backwards on 'I'm Only Sleeping', or spitting blistering distortion on the glorious ensemble work of 'And Your Bird Can Sing' and fuelling Paul's superb solo on 'Taxman'. As a contrast, the group could conjure such tranquil gems as the two ghostly guitar 'statements' on 'Here, There And Everywhere' which sound like George's Rick 12-string, possibly played through a Leslie rotating speaker.

Later in the year the group played their last concerts, in Germany, Japan, The Philippines and the US. John and George mainly used the Casinos, George also taking a Rick 12, while the SG and a J-160 went along as back-ups. Paul played the familiar Höfner bass, with a Rickenbacker 4001S bass he'd acquired in 1965 as back-up. But *Revolver* had made it clear

▽ JOHN LENNON'S EPIPHONE CASINO E-230-TD
Casino produced 1961-1969; this example c1965

Following Paul's earlier purchase, John and George each acquired a Casino during 1966, ready to use on the studio sessions for the Revolver album as well as live dates at the time.

▽ PAUL McCARTNEY'S EPIPHONE CASINO E-230-TDB
Casino produced 1961-1969; this example November 1962

Paul's interest in six-string studio work beyond his bold bass led to him securing this Epiphone Casino in 1964, soon used on tracks like 'Ticket to Ride' and 'Paperback Writer'. It wasn't the most expensive Epi available in Britain then, but Paul chose a Casino because UK importer Rosetti offered it with a Bigsby vibrato option. "It's a bit of a cheap Gibson, actually," Paul said recently, "but I loved the Bigsby – Eddie Cochran used to have one. If I had to choose one electric guitar, it would be this."

JOHN on-stage with his Casino (left). Later he stripped the paint off to reveal the natural wood, which is how the guitar remains today in the care of Yoko Ono (above). By necessity Paul always played bass on-stage with The Beatles, but is seen in the studio with his Casino on the cover of this 1968 magazine (right).

BEAT INSTRUMENTAL SEPT. 3/-

London in late 1962 and early 1963, one can hear George's Gretsch and John's Rickenbacker, over Paul's Höfner 'violin' bass (by now Paul was, of course, the group's bassman).

George and John had each bought a Gibson J-160E electric-acoustic guitar from a local Liverpool music store, Rushworth's, in September 1962. These filled a gap in their instrumental set-up. Essentially traditional round-soundhole acoustics but with a pickup and controls built in, the big Gibsons – known as 'the jumbos' by the group – could be used unplugged as straightforward acoustic guitars for songwriting on the road and for studio work, or plugged-in to give an amplified approximation of an acoustic guitar for softer numbers on stage or in the studio.

Probably the following month John had the natural-look wood of his Rickenbacker refinished in black. Perhaps this was to match George's black Gretsch, or simply to hide some damage. At the time Kevin Swift wrote in *Beat Instrumental*: "Fans who had got used to the sight of John's brown Rickenbacker now saw him belting away at three pickups, a scratchplate and control knobs which seemed to be hanging in mid air. Explanation? The new black finish got lost against his dark clothes."

George got another Gretsch at this time, probably at the end of 1963. It was a Tennessean model, similar to his Country Gent but with a single cutaway and single-coil pickups. The Tennessean saw much service, and was used by George interchangeably with the Country Gent for recording sessions through to the end of 1965 – *A Hard Day's Night*, *Beatles For Sale*, *Help!* and *Rubber Soul* – as well as contemporary live work. Both Gibson jumbos also saw a lot of use over this period. In fact, at the end of 1963 one of the Gibsons had been stolen during a performance in north London, and was quickly replaced.

The day before that pivotal TV broadcast from New York in February 1964 during The Beatles' first American visit, Francis Hall, the boss of the Rickenbacker company, had come over specially to the East Coast from California to show the group some new gear. It was an inspired move that would earn Rickenbacker untold sales during the 1960s and well beyond. As a result of Rickenbacker's foresight, George ended up with a fabulous gift of the company's brand new 12-string electric, while John would be given a gleaming new-look version of his 325 model.

A week later in Florida John took delivery of his new black Rickenbacker, with its distinctive white pickguard and five-knob control layout, in time to use for a further *Ed Sullivan* TV appearance, after which it became his main instrument. George waited until their return to England to use his new toy, and the studio debut of both his chiming 12-string and John's soloing 325 can be heard on the exuberant 'You Can't Do That', recorded on George's 21st birthday.

that the studio was now the outlet for The Beatles' creativity, and at the end of 1966 they started sessions for what would become *Sgt Pepper's Lonely Hearts Club Band*.

A reporter for *The Beatles Book* magazine witnessed the studio overflowing with musical hardware. "The Beatles play far more instruments [now]," he wrote. "The total count at the moment is 14 guitars, a tambura, one sitar, a two-manual Vox organ, and Ringo's Ludwig kit, plus various pianos and organs supplied by EMI." Those 14 guitars would probably have included John's recently acquired Gretsch Nashville and certainly Paul's new Fender Esquire. Fenders dominated the few conventional guitar solos on offer during *Pepper* – the attractively frenetic contribution by McCartney and Esquire to 'Good Morning Good Morning', and George's hollow-toned, detuned, double-tracked Strat on 'Fixing A Hole'. Staccato Fenders probably power 'Getting Better', too, and the Leslie speaker is employed to colour John's ensemble guitar on 'Lucy In The Sky With Diamonds'.

In a way the guitars themselves had become less important to the group. Studio treatments and unusual colourings were now in demand from whatever source. To fill the increasingly diverse aural picture sounds and timbres were actively sought from all manner of tape sources and instruments, including orchestras and brass sections and Mellotrons.

Around the time they recorded and filmed *Magical Mystery Tour*, with its central character of a dayglo-painted coach, the group, imbued with the hippy-trippy spirit of the times,

decided to paint a few of their instruments in wildly psychedelic colour schemes. Paul decorated his Rickenbacker bass, George got out the spray-cans and attacked his Stratocaster, while John had his jumbo painted blue, red and purple, and sprayed the back of his Casino silver. "We did the cars too," Paul told me recently. "If you did the cars, you might as well do your guitars. It looked great, and it was just because we were tripping. That's what it was, man. Look at your guitar and you'd trip even more." Later – perhaps in a fit of post-trip good taste – Paul and John had the paint stripped off the coloured guitars, down to the natural wood, but George's Strat stayed steadfastly psychedelic.

By the time of the sessions in 1968 for '*The White Album*' the sound of the group's electric guitars had become heavier and more distorted, often stacked up in great riffing slabs ('Birthday') or piled on in sheets of punctuating accents ('Happiness Is A Warm Gun'). It becomes more difficult to pick out individual contributions, although the renowned solo by Eric Clapton on 'While My Guitar Gently Weeps' is unmistakable enough. Eric gave George the red Les Paul that he'd used for that wonderful piece of work, and it may well be this guitar that George uses for the distant, dejected moaning at the end of 'Sexy Sadie'.

Certainly when it came to *Let It Be* and *Abbey Road*, in 1969, George was using the Les Paul. He also got a new Fender Rosewood Telecaster around the time of *Let It Be*,

which he can be seen playing on the famous Apple rooftop concert in the film. (Fender gave some other instruments to the group at the same time, including a six-string bass and a couple of Fender-Rhodes pianos.) The Les Paul can be heard on George's rather-too-careful solo slotted into 'Something', while his heavy Tele turns up on the album version (fuzz solo) and single version (Leslie'd solo) of 'Let It Be'.

On *Abbey Road* there is some strong competition for the guitars from the fresh sounds of the group's newly discovered Moog synthesiser, but the record's parting shot is, in effect, a guitar set-piece: 'The End'. Paul, George and John, in that order, each take a two-bar solo, cycling around three times. Paul's brittle tone suggests his Esquire; George's work is pure wailing Les Paul; John makes an aggressive, distorted howl with his Casino. And that, apart from 'Her Majesty', is that.

It had been quite a journey from the late 1950s when the boys got their first guitars. George explained in 1964: "I started to learn to play when I was 13 on an old Spanish model which my dad picked up for 50 bob (£2.50, about $4). It's funny how little things can change your life. Don't ask me why he chose a guitar instead of a mouth organ or something – they certainly weren't popular at the time." As it turned out, George and The Beatles were responsible not only for creating some utterly magical and simply timeless music, but for doing much to make the electric guitar the most popular musical instrument of the 1960s. ■ TONY BACON

FENDER guitars did not become part of the Beatles' guitar line-up until 1965 when George and John acquired a sonic blue Strat each. Paul too picked up an Esquire a year or two later. Why did they wait so long? Perhaps in part it was a reaction against the Fender-toting, old-guard Shadows. But in 1967 George made 'Rocky' an even more personal friend with this psychedelic-cum-rockability paint job.

GEORGE is pictured in the EMI studios at Abbey Road (left) with his painted Strat during the recording of 'Revolution' on 4th June 1968. On the back of a 1969 edition of The Beatles Book (above) George is seen with the Rosewood Telecaster that he played on the famous Apple rooftop concert in the group's 1970 film Let It Be.

△ GEORGE HARRISON'S GIBSON LES PAUL
Les Paul produced 1952-current: this example 1957

This famous Les Paul was a gift from Eric Clapton after he'd used it to record the majestic guitar solo for The Beatles track 'While My Guitar Gently Weeps' in September 1968. When Clapton acquired the guitar it had already been refinished red; the instrument's re-stamped serial number corresponds to an entry in Gibson's log for a shipment of a Les Paul, implicitly a gold-top, to one Gartner Sweet on 19th December 1957.

△ DOMINO CALIFORNIA REBEL
Produced 1967-1968; this example 1967

Maurice Lipsky, a distributor based in New York, imported guitars from various Japanese makers for his Domino line. This original and relatively high-quality example was probably made by Kawai. Oddities abound: note the elegant f-hole (it surmounts a sound cavity cut into the solid body), the Spanish-style slotted headstock, and edge "binding" which is painted on.

HANK GARLAND *(left) was a country session player based in Nashville who put his distinctive stamp on 45s such as Elvis Presley's 'Little Sister' and Don Gibson's 'Sea Of* Heartbreak' *(with Chet Atkins). In 1960 Garland recorded this jazz-flavoured LP (left), but the following year the 31-year-old was injured in a car crash that effectively ended his career.*

COUNTRY GUITARS

It was the 1960s and change was the big thing, both in and outside music. And those ten years saw country guitars and guitarists not only receiving musical currents from outside the hillbilly universe, but also serving as prime influences on the fast-developing pop music scene.

As the 1960s began, mega-stars like Jim Reeves were making mellow, pop-influenced tunes, including 'He'll Have To Go' with the brilliant Hank Garland offering only the most understated of backings on his Gibson hollow-body. Within a year Garland would release the riveting *Jazz Winds From A New Direction*, a whirlwind of high-level improvisation. The album cover shows him with an actual convertible full of Gibsons. Then, in mid-decade, the most popular group in the world featured Ringo Starr wailing Buck Owens' 'Act Naturally' – with Beatle George Harrison's hollow-body Gretsch doing its best to mimic one of country's hottest sounds, the trebly twang of Buck Owens & The Buckaroos' Telecasters. And by the end of the 1960s country-rockers such as the newly-energised Byrds were assembling Dylan-inspired songwriting, crisp California picking and Everlys-style harmonies for an enduring new sound.

But back to the beginning. Country music had survived the body blow dealt to it by Elvis and rock'n'roll by developing the smooth, widely palatable Nashville Sound. In the studios of Nashville, this meant that a small cast of musical movers and shakers were kept wildly busy, sometimes recording for as long as 15 hours a day. "We could do four sessions a day: 10am, 2pm, 6pm and 10pm," recalls the great session guitarist Harold Bradley, referring to the standardised times for three-hour studio sessions. "If you were booked solid for four sessions, they'd say, 'We'll start at 1.30 in the morning.' They demanded it!" Bradley laughs. "The artists would say: 'We're not gonna cut it without you guys.'"

The pressure was intense to come up with great performances every time. The need for new and distinctive sounds meant players and producers were constantly on the lookout for new tools and techniques. In one famous incident the recording crew at Music Row's renowned Quonset Hut studio got creative when a malfunctioning pre-amp in the recording console produced a wild, evenly distorted sound. Making use of the sound was session great Grady Martin, who produced the famed distortion-powered solo on six-string bass for Marty Robbins' 1961 hit 'Don't Worry'. As that record puzzled and then captivated listeners in the pop and country fields, the fuzztone era was under way. "Later when I found out what it was, I set about trying to develop that sound using transistors," recalls veteran engineer Glenn Snoddy. "We fooled around with it and got the sound like we wanted. I drove up to Chicago and presented it to Mr Berlin, the boss at the Gibson company, and he heard that it was something different. So they agreed to take it and put it out as a commercial product." The result was the first off-the-shelf fuzzbox, the Gibson Maestro.

Early echo effects like the tape-derived Ecco-Fonic and Gibson's Echoplex began to see wide use in the early 1960s, with Hank Garland making it part of his identifiable sound on records by Patsy Cline and others. Mr Guitar, Chet Atkins, continued to unleash a variety of sounds, even as he became more and more involved as a producer. Sales of his Gretsch models soared with their use by Harrison, who featured Chet-style licks on Fabs hits like 'All My Loving'. Guitars from other makers, such as the Gibson ES series and Fender's Jazzmaster that had been developed at the end of the 1950s, enjoyed increasing use in the Nashville studios by the early 1960s.

"When I started with Jim Reeves, I had a big Gibson ES-5,"

SALESMEN look glum on the La Baye stand at a 1967 trade show (right): not one of the new 2-By-4 models was sold. The same year at a British show, Vox designer Dick Denney (far right) demos their Winchester small-body guitar. Below him, Dave Roberts tries a multi-control Vox Marauder.

△ LA BAYE 2-BY-4
Produced 1967; this example 1967

Dan Helland had a great idea. Why bother to have a body on a solid electric guitar? In theory it could be anything, so why not make it a piece of two-by-four? In typical 1960s fashion, odd theory became strange practice. Helland met guitar manufacturer Holman-Woodell (who had already made instruments for Wurlitzer as well as their own Holman brand), and La Baye was set up in Green Bay, Wisconsin. The plan got no further than prototypes at a trade show, and while some later 2-By-4s turned up branded 21st Century, no more than 90 in total are thought to have been produced, making this a rare sample of 1960s frivolity.

MESSENGER's guitar (right) used a one-piece magnesium alloy chassis that combined headstock, neck and body extension. This use of the structural strength of metal was new for guitars. Messenger explained that it permitted a neck that was thin "from first to 21st fret", as well as a fingerboard completely free of the body, allowing superb top-fret access. The guitar was also stereo-wired. However, this plethora of attributes failed to attract players, and not many Messengers were delivered.

△ MESSENGER ME-11
Produced 1967; this example 1967

Another 1960s maker destined for obscurity, Messenger made guitars with a structural "backbone" of magnesium alloy. This example has been refinished from its original sunburst to green.

JIM REEVES (above, centre) was the most successful 1960s example of how the Nashville Sound crossed over into easy-listening pop-hit territory. Leo

Jackson, guitarist in Reeves' backing group The Blue Boys, smiles (second from left) as they take delivery of a truckload of suitably blue-finished

Rickenbacker gear in 1961. However, Jackson was more often to be seen with his Jazzmaster (right), also with a special blue-boy paint job.

says long-time Reeves sideman and session musician Leo Jackson. "But I saw this guy play a Fender one time and it just knocked me out, the guy got so much out of the guitar. I said, 'I'm going to get me one of them.'" Jackson bought a Strat in 1957, but switched to a Jazzmaster by the time he accompanied Reeves on hits like 'Distant Drums' and 'I Love You Because'. There was one drawback to playing with Reeves. The singer took the name of his Blue Boys band seriously, and had Jackson spray his Fender Jazzmaster light blue with automobile paint.

A leading light of the sessions scene, Grady Martin worked zillions of dates on his famous ES-355 named Big Red, which had palm pedals to create steel-guitar-like pitch shifts. "I had an ES-335 that I bought down at Hewgley's store in 1961. That was the guitar of choice with those [session] guys," recalls guitarist-producer Jerry Kennedy, whose melodic playing appeared on countless hits such as Tammy Wynette's 'Stand By Your Man' and Roy Orbison's 'Pretty Woman'. Kennedy recalled: "A guy named Dean Porter put those string-benders on my 335 – one lever that lowered the E-string down a tone and one that raised the second [B-] string a whole tone. Now, I wish I'd had them put on some other guitar." Session player/executive Kelso Herston recalls getting an ES-345 "because Hank Garland had one".

Though Gibsons and Fenders remained the key country instruments for much of the 1960s, other makes popped up all

GEORGE HARRISON's use of a sitar on 'Norwegian Wood' in 1965 led everybody to want one on their record. "The trouble is they are difficult to tune and obtain," sessionman Jimmy Page told a reporter. An electric sitar was needed: the Rajah from 1967 (right) was a false start; the winner proved to be the Coral Sitar (below).

△ CORAL SITAR
Produced 1967-1970; this example c1968

This electric sitar brought the exotic sounds of the complicated Indian instrument to guitar players. The key to the Sitar's imitation of the Indian sound was its "flat" plastic bridge, designed by session guitarist Vinnie Bell to give just the right buzzy edge... but it also meant the Sitar was virtually impossible to keep in tune. Coral was another brandname used by the New Jersey-based guitar manufacturer, Danelectro, after it was bought by MCA in 1967.

Vincent Bell SIGNATURE DESIGN ELECTRIC SITAR

BUCK OWENS (above right) and his guitarist Don Rich (left) spearheaded the Tele's popularity in 1960s country music after Fender gave them each a silver-sparkle model.

the time. Thumbs Carllile played a Mosrite electric dobro, session regular Chip Young had a Rickenbacker electric with palm pedals, and Harold Bradley was one of the first to try the Coral electric sitar. Baldwin, eager to get in on the Nashville scene, gave several key players some electric models, which were rarely used. Kelso Herston played the rampaging solo on George Jones' 'The Race Is On' on a Danelectro six-string bass, getting a startling sound by using lots of echo and an early in-studio phasing effect – more than three years before The Small Faces' celebrated phase-laden 'Itchycoo Park'. Herston's playing on the Jones record was pure twang. "I guess probably it was a steal from the West Coast. Don Rich and all those guys out there were doing it, so we just did it an octave lower," he recalls.

Bradley kept an enormous assortment of guitars in a room known as the 'closet' of the Quonset Hut. Included was his Jazzmaster that was passed around by many of the studio masters of the day. "Hank Garland was playing a Gibson and he called me," Bradley says. "He said, 'My guitar doesn't twang like yours. I've got this Elvis session coming up:

CHET ATKINS worked hard to establish the Nashville Sound in the 1960s, both as a record producer and guitarist. As a well-respected professional, Atkins' continued use of Gretsch guitars (Country Gentleman, above) did much for that company's image.

ELECTRIC SITAR proved to be an irresistible flavour for many late-1960s record producers. Inventor Vinnie Bell played his Coral Sitar on many East-coast records, such as Joe South's 'Games People Play', and 'Green Tambourine' by The Lemon Pipers (left). Al Nichol of The Turtles (centre) was another enthusiastic Sitar player, using it here for one of the group's many live shows.

VINNIE BELL was a session guitarist who spotted a demand for trendy sitar sounds in New York studios in the mid 1960s. Bell had already worked with Danelectro in 1961 to design their early electric 12-string, the Bellzouki model, and his Coral Sitar was launched by the company in 1967. Bell shamelessly appeared in a turban (left) that year to publicise the new instrument. As well as a special "buzzy" bridge the Sitar had 13 extra drone strings with a separate pickup and controls to assist the sitar impersonation.

△ GALANTI GRAND PRIX 3003
Produced c1967-1968; this example c1967

Italian makers had moved on from the wilder excesses of the early 1960s (see Wandre, page 24) to produce more sober and approachable models such as this decent instrument, imported into the US by Galanti. Nonetheless, accordion influence remains in the pushbutton selector strip.

can I borrow your Fender?'" The session was on June 26th 1961, the tune was Presley's 'Little Sister', and the guitar part's trebly, bluesy tone prompted many imitators. Presley, recording for RCA in Nashville at the time, was only one of a slew of pop artists who hit town to make use of the casual but highly creative session scene on Music Row.

Meanwhile, pop of a different kind had worked its way into country through the innovations of a young Buck Owens. His country roots and his wide-ranging interests in other styles married and gave birth to The Twang. "I think that probably came from playing 'Jenny Jenny Jenny' and 'Tutti Frutti' and those things," remembers Owens, who freely mixed rock and country during his years of playing the honky-tonks in Bakersfield, California. The treble-heavy sound of the guitar's low end was a necessity because Owens had to work hard to be heard over the noisy night-life crowd. The sound also gave a nod to the kind of tone popularised by pop guitarists such as Duane Eddy and The Ventures' Nokie Edwards (the latter of whom worked with Owens for a while).

Seldom has an artist been more closely associated with a guitar than Buck Owens and the Telecaster. In 1963 the Fender company presented him and his guitarist Don Rich with

MERLE HAGGARD was an ideally named country star. His tough, real-life songs celebrated the downtrodden, drawing on his own unruly youth and prison spells.

Haggard's group The Strangers included guitarist Roy Nichols who produced an inventive Tele-driven mix of string abuse, heard to great effect on the 1967 album pictured above.

matching crushed-mirror sparkle-finish chequered-binding Teles. The act returned the favour by featuring them on a string of huge, hard-hitting records – including 'Act Naturally', later covered by The Beatles. An amazing nine of *Billboard*'s Top 50 US singles of the decade were by Buck and the Buckaroos. "When Buck came out with 'Tiger By The Tail' [in 1965] there was a big revival of Fender," Bradley says.

Out in California the honky-tonk strains begun in the 1950s by Tommy Collins, Wynn Stewart and others came to full flower as Owens and then Merle Haggard came up with hit after hit based on true-life heartache and guitaristics of a wholly new sort. West Coasters including Phil Baugh, James Burton and Roy Nichols were twisting strings, choking strings, slapping strings and chicken-picking strings in ways that arose organically out of the solidbody, highly-responsive Tele.

"I remember going down for the first session on a song that we were working on," Haggard says. "Roy Nichols and I were sitting on the steps of my little old apartment and talking about the necessity of having some kind of different guitar style – something that people like and remember and identify with," Haggard says. "And I remember Roy said, 'What would happen if a guy took the string and pushed it up and then hit

THE BYRDS *changed dramatically in 1968. Gram Parsons joined briefly, steering the group to a new course that resulted in one of the period's most influential country-rock LPs,* Sweetheart Of The Rodeo *(left). Bluegrass/country picker Clarence White (right) was also added to the line-up; his steely Tele was another vital element in The Byrds' new sound.*

it and let it come down, rather than hitting it while it's going up?' I said, 'Let me see what you mean.' He showed me, and that was the beginning of the Merle Haggard style, coming down with the guitar string."

The 1966 Hag hit 'I'm A Lonesome Fugitive' finds Nichols chicken-picking, bending those notes down after they're hit, and popping the strings in a totally electric technique that was riveting and hit-making. James Burton, who had started making the Tele famous as a teenage sideman to Ricky Nelson, created mind-twisting licks on many of the early Haggard sessions on his way to becoming one of country's and pop's most revered twangmasters. Burton eventually joined Elvis Presley's touring band in 1969. Meanwhile, The Beatles

weren't the only pop acts tuning into country music, guitarists and guitars. The Lovin' Spoonful paid tribute to the innumerable pickers of Music City in the 1966 hit 'Nashville Cats', while Bob Dylan started a major wave of pop stars to Nashville studios beginning with his sessions there for the 1966 rock masterpiece *Blonde On Blonde*. More significantly, he came back to record the groundbreaking country records *John Wesley Harding* (1968) and *Nashville Skyline* (1969) with a new breed of Nashville picker that included studio session guitarists such as Wayne Moss, Joe South and Charlie Daniels.

Virtually single-handedly, Dylan focused the interest of the rock community on country studios and players. Of course, as

Daniels notes, "Any rock musician worth his salt has an awful lot of respect for country music – and it's been that way for a long time. How can you help from liking George Jones?" Wielding a stock 1966 Telecaster he bought in Maine during his years as a rock'n'roll journeyman, Daniels put his feisty, aggressive stamp on Dylan tunes like 'Country Pie' as well as playing a string of other country and folk sessions.

In the second half of the 1960s the cutting edge of country was definitely picking and singing its way out of California. Owens was king of country radio and Haggard was well on his way to becoming one of country's all-time innovators and creative models. And then came country-rock. As early as 1966 The Byrds had included the hillbilly anthem 'Satisfied Mind' on their *Turn Turn Turn* LP, with former folkies Jim (later Roger) McGuinn and David Crosby plus former bluegrasser Chris Hillman melding vocal harmonies and jangling

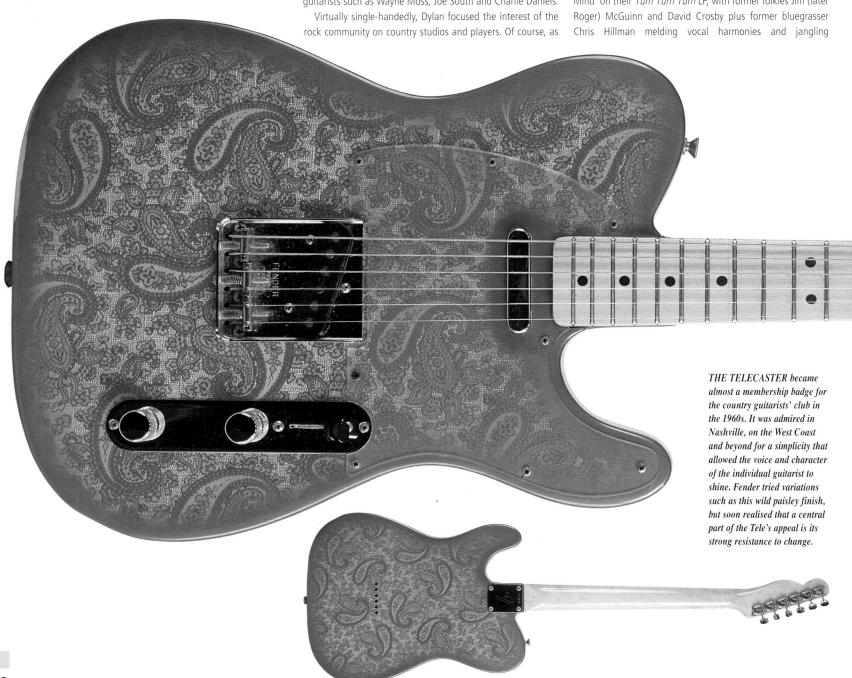

THE TELECASTER *became almost a membership badge for the country guitarists' club in the 1960s. It was admired in Nashville, on the West Coast and beyond for a simplicity that allowed the voice and character of the individual guitarist to shine. Fender tried variations such as this wild paisley finish, but soon realised that a central part of the Tele's appeal is its strong resistance to change.*

BOB DYLAN highlighted the move of many pop musicians toward country by making two LPs in Nashville in the late 1960s: John Wesley Harding, and Nashville Skyline (sleeve, far left). Before that, in an enforced retreat, Dylan had hidden away with The Band to record a series of demos. The Band's debut album Music From Big Pink (left) appeared in 1968, and it too drew on country as well as folk and rock, creating an atmospheric slice of Americana.

JAMES BURTON was one of the best-known session guitarists of the 1960s. He had come to fame in the 1950s and early 1960s working with Ricky Nelson (right), but in the mid 1960s began to play more country-oriented sessions for the likes of Merle Haggard and Buck Owens. For his 1969 solo album (below) he teamed up with pedal-steel man Ralph Mooney. A big Tele fan, Burton

later swapped this red one for a Paisley Red example which he used as a member of Elvis Presley's band in the 1970s.

Rickenbackers in the beginnings of a new sound. Even The Rolling Stones recorded Hank Snow's 'I'm Moving On', and The Beatles continued to release countrified tunes like 'I've Just Seen a Face' and 'What Goes On'. Then in 1968 came two

Rick Nelson and James Burton play

landmark records: The Byrds' all-country *Sweetheart Of The Rodeo* and The Band's country-tinged debut album, *Music From Big Pink*. Psychedelia had serious competition. The Byrds continued in a country vein throughout the rest of the 1960s, losing Hillman and Parsons to The Flying Burrito Brothers, but gaining the great guitarist Clarence White. Beginning his career as a groundbreaking bluegrasser, White became a Telecaster blaster under the tutelage of James Burton, appearing in early country-rock bands as well as developing a strap-activated string bender, still available today, along with Byrd-mate Gene Parsons.

From those country-rock roots came a host of bands. It began with Poco and culminated in the 1970s with the Eagles, who in a turnabout went on to influence mainstream country music well into the 1990s. "We definitely ruffled some feathers down there, but nothing collapsed, nothing went away," Byrds bassist Chris Hillman recalled years later of the group's 1968 appearance at the Grand Ole Opry. "We didn't destroy any tradition. People just weren't exactly ready to have a West Coast rock band on that stage."

Far from destroying tradition, the 1960s marriage of country and rock produced a vital form that, in its best incarnations, still enriches both styles. And as the century ends, the twangin' guitar sound that powered the 1960s airwaves remains as stylish as the ever-popular Telecaster. ■ TOMMY GOLDSMITH

MARTIN LUTHER KING is shot dead in Memphis, and Senator Robert Kennedy is assassinated in Los Angeles.

2001: A SPACE ODYSSEY has Sixties audiences enthralled by its sweeping tale from ape-man to space station, its trip-like visuals and its enigmatic message. One review describes the 140-minute movie as "somewhere between hypnotic and immensely boring".

FRENCH STUDENTS riot and heavy street fighting ensues. Workers call a general strike in support and the country comes to a halt. Elections are called amid new riots, but the Gaullists hold power, defeating the Communists in a landslide.

BLACK ATHLETES give controversial black-power salutes at a Mexico Olympics awards ceremony.

THE VIETCONG mount the "Tet Offensive", a series of continued attacks on the South Vietnamese capital, Saigon. This calls into question the ability of South Vietnamese and US forces to win the war.

SOVIET and Warsaw Pact forces invade increasingly liberal Czechoslovakia, re-imposing totalitarianism. A treaty is signed providing for Soviet troops to be stationed in Czechoslovakia, which becomes a two-state federation.

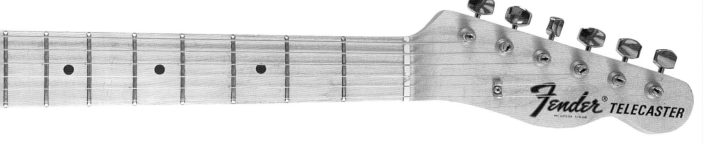

△ FENDER PAISLEY RED TELECASTER
Produced 1968-1969; this example 1968

This guitar shouts "Sixties!" louder than almost any other in the book, thanks to Fender's bold attempt to turn an ordinary Telecaster into a far-out psychedelic art object. Collectors would have you believe that after Fender were taken over by CBS in 1965 they became boring; clearly they do not have a paisley Tele in their collection. Fender simply went to the local wallpaper store and picked this Paisley Red design (as well as a Blue Flower pattern, left) from the self-adhesive line. Back at the factory, instead of painting Teles they stuck on the wallpaper.

FENDER's Telecaster was the least likely target for Paisley Red (opposite) and Blue Flower finishes (flyer, left). Since its launch in 1951 the Tele was rarely seen without its standard blond finish, even though custom colours were offered.

63

ARIA is one of many Japanese guitar brands of the 1960s that lasted for decades beyond. Aria guitars first appeared in Japan in 1956, with electrics launched around 1960. This 1968 catalogue (left) reflects the popularity of hollow-body electrics at the time, inspired by The Beatles who went on stage with Epiphones, Rickenbackers and Höfners in Tokyo in 1966.

△ ARIA DIAMOND ADSG-12T
Produced c1968-1969; this example c1968

By the late 1960s Japanese makers had absorbed many Western influences. This guitar has the Fender-inspired "offset waist" body shape that so many manufacturers found appealing. It also shows that the craze for electric 12-string guitars lasted longer in Japan – by 1968 in America and Europe the jingle-jangle sound was in decline from its first peak of popularity. The Arai company used two brands: Aria, and (as here) Aria Diamond.

SHIRO ARAI (above) was a keen classical guitarist and the president of Arai, the company which made Aria guitars.

64

THE BLUE JEANS (right) were one of the most revered Japanese groups of the 1960s; their guitarist, Takeshi Terauchi, became famous among young hopefuls, who nicknamed him "God's Hands" thanks to the divine inspiration that fired his fretwork. The Blue Jeans, along with other Japanese groups such as The Out Cast, The Spiders, The Playboys and Swing West, created a uniquely Eastern interpretation of a wild Ventures/Beatles guitar mix.

YUZO KAYAMA (left) did much to popularise electric guitars in Japan in the 1960s, selling many records and appearing in a movie that dramatised the electric guitar boom. Kayama was rarely seen without his white Mosrite Ventures model six-string, highlighting the overwhelming popularity of both the group and the guitar in Japan.

JAPANESE GUITARS

In Japan there was no escaping the guitar in the 1960s. First there was The Ventures-inspired electric guitar boom, and then the Group Sounds fad triggered by The Beatles. Guitars became so popular that one education committee even banned them, fearful of their effect on the nation's youth. But Japan's factories poured out thousands upon thousands of guitars for a hungry domestic market – as well as for equally demanding importers in Europe, the US and elsewhere – and brandnames such as Aria, Ibanez and Yamaha made their first impressions on young guitarists around the world.

As the 1960s got underway the popularity of the guitar in America and Europe continued to grow. With an increasing number of teenage guitar players, these countries couldn't keep up with the demand on their own, and began to buy increasing numbers of instruments from exporting countries such as Japan.

During the late 1950s and into the early 1960s only Teisco and Guyatone exported electric guitars from Japan to the US and Europe. These two companies had begun producing electric musical instruments soon after World War II, gaining experience through exports. Into the early 1960s, with the instrumental surf music trend in America, this trade grew, and by 1962 Teisco and Guyatone were overwhelmed by orders.

American musical instrument importers in particular flocked to Japan, looking for new manufacturers. They visited guitar factories and offered manufacturers the chance to develop and export electric guitars. These Japanese makers didn't really have the expertise to make electric guitars, but the importers brought with them brochures and American-made guitars to demonstrate what an electric guitar should be like. Some manufacturers showed an interest and took on development, somehow managing to make guitar-like products and export solid electric instruments, as dictated by the importers.

Despite their relative lack of knowledge, these companies passionately devoted themselves to develop and learn the production techniques and very quickly were setting up mass-production systems. The Japanese manufacturers who started to produce electric guitars in this way in the early 1960s included Fujigen Gakki which made guitars with Goya, Kent and other importer brands, and Kawai Gakki, whose brands included Kawai, Domino, Kingston, Heit and Winston. Also in operation were the Arai Trading Company (Aria and Aria Diamond brands), Zen-on Gakki (Zenon, Morales), Hoshino Gakki (Ibanez, Star) and Kasuga Gakki (Mellowtone).

In 1964 surf music finally reached the shores of Japan. Songs by The Astronauts and similar groups arrived and instrumental surf music gradually grew in popularity. But the one group which caught the hearts and minds of the young Japanese was The Ventures. That year the group released two singles in Japan, 'Walk – Don't Run, 64' and 'Diamond Head', which launched their oriental success. The Ventures' Japanese tour in January 1965 triggered an unprecedented electric

guitar boom. The kids who heard The Ventures' music lost their hearts to the wild sound of electric guitars, rushed to the music stores to buy the records – and many decided to start groups of their own. One of the most successful was The Blue Jeans, led by Takeshi Terauchi, who had one electric instrumental hit after another. Young fans of the electric guitar were transfixed by Terauchi, who because of his stunning technique was nicknamed God's Hands.

Another popular guitarist was Yuzo Kayama. He made TV and concert appearances with a white Mosrite as his main instrument, and his records sold very well. Kayama, who had originally been an actor, also starred in a crucially important movie called *Eleki No Wakadaisho* (which means something like "Japanese Electric Guitar Explosion"). The film had a storyline based on the electric guitar boom, and itself helped to expand the market still further. During 1965 demand in Japan for electric guitars rose rapidly and manufacturers finally started to focus on domestic sales.

The two established companies, Teisco and Guyatone, were leading the industry in 1960s Japan, competing as friendly rivals and constantly unveiling new models. In 1962 Teisco's line consisted primarily of cheap plywood solidbody guitars, including the MJ, SD, SS and WG series. Designs were full of originality, and from 1964 Teisco began to sell better quality models. These included the TG-64 (featured in *Eleki No Wakadaisho*) which had a 'grip hole' in the body, and the TRG-1 with a built-in speaker.

Guyatone had the solidbody LG series at the start of the 1960s, and in 1963 marketed the popular LG-65T model and the hollow-body electric Musician. Two years later they announced what is arguably their best-ever model, the LG-200T.

△ TEISCO DEL REY MAY QUEEN
Produced c1968-1969; this example c1968

In America the big takeover story of the 1960s was Fender's purchase by CBS in 1965. Two years later came Japan's equivalent when Kawai bought Teisco, who were in trouble from investing in stock that was not selling. In 1968 the revamped Teisco began to produce a new line of electric guitars, including this May Queen model that followed the Japanese trend of the time for hollow-body electrics. The eccentric body shape was influenced by Vox's Mando Guitar of 1967, a sort of short-scale 12-string solidbody mandolin.

JAPANESE guitar makers began to export in greater numbers as the guitar boom hit in the early 1960s. Some even advertised directly in American trade magazines (1964 example, left) offering US distributors the opportunity to buy guitars more cheaply than the most budget-priced home-made products. Some had relatively original designs, while others later copied more closely the general shapes – if not the fine detail – of the best-selling Western instruments.

65

KENT's 742 was a top-of-the-line Japanese stunner, with a figured maple body and enough pickups and controls to satisfy the most knob-crazy gadget freak. Each pickup has an on/off switch, plus a volume and tone control below.

Guyatone's LG-200T was an epoch-making instrument: it had 24 frets, stereo circuitry, and enabled various sound combinations from four pickups and six selector switches.

As the electric guitar boom took off in 1965 still more brandnames appeared on the scene, including Columbia, Elk, Mory, Pleasant, Splender, Suzuki, Tombo, Victor, Voice, and Zen-on. Among these, Pleasant and Zen-on were already exporters, but now they unveiled many new products with the accent on domestic sales.

Elk started off as an amplifier manufacturer in 1963. Because its founder, Yukiho Yamada, was an active steel guitar player, the company enjoyed a strong connection with professional musicians in Japan, and offered a top-notch, high-quality product line. In 1965 they began producing electric guitars, and from the beginning aimed at making accurate, good-quality Fender copies. One of Elk's first models was the Deluxe, a Fender Jaguar-style solidbody that was highly acclaimed by Japanese professionals.

Voice, on the other hand, manufactured small-volume, high-quality handbuilt guitars. Its founder, Yukichi Iwase, had worked for Teisco as an engineer. In 1964 his new company started to develop electric guitars and the following year released the Frontier Custom 1000. Thanks to the engineering skills and elaborate handmaking techniques he'd nurtured at

Teisco, Iwase built a guitar that was accepted by a number of professional musicians, and later by a wider public.

In many cases what was intended for export was also sold domestically, retaining the overseas customer's brand. This makes it difficult to calculate how many brands were available in Japan in the 1960s, but it was probably over 30. Some manufacturers expanded their business for export, and 1965 saw the whole industry devoting itself to the production of electric guitars.

Makers at this time enthusiastically introduced new models. Structurally, these instruments were strongly influenced by Fender, and in design and mechanical operation by Burns, Harmony, Framus, Eko and others, with each maker trying to project originality. As we've seen, at first in the 1960s Japanese-made guitars were intended for export, and destined to copy popular products – at least partly due to requests from the overseas distributors themselves. But from 1965 many makers instead of manufacturing faithful copies attempted to absorb only the best points of foreign products while pursuing their own original designs.

TV broadcasts in 1965 included electric guitar programmes with audience participation, such as *Kachinuki Eleki Gassen* ("Electric Guitar Tournament"), and guitar competitions were held throughout the country. The Ventures came to Japan for

ELECTRIC GUITARS were considered harmful influences on 1960s Japanese youth, and precautions were taken. This newspaper cutting (below) from 1965 reports a banning of electric guitars by the Ashikaga city education committee.

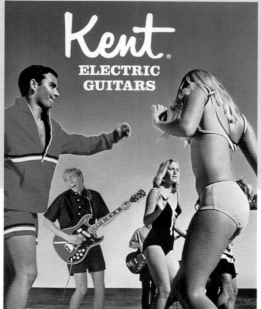

▽ KENT 742
Produced c1968-1969; this example c1968

Kent was a brandname applied by leading New York-based instrument wholesaler Buegeleisen & Jacobson to its imported line of Japanese-made guitars. At first Kents were manufactured by Guyatone, but in 1967 B&J changed supplier, probably to Kawai. This magnificent multi-control four-pickup Kent is from the new source. (The vibrato and bridge here are not original.)

▽ KAWAI CONCERT
Produced c1968-1970; this example c1968

By the end of the decade Kawai was one of the biggest guitar makers in Japan, producing instruments for the domestic market with its own brandname as well as supplying many export customers in the US and Europe. The Concert, looking more like some kind of oriental weapon than a guitar, was one of Kawai's most distinctive models.

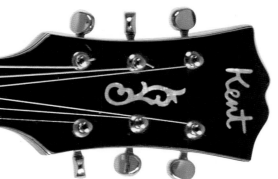

a second time and toured nationally for a month, ensuring the continued popularity of electric guitars. For many Japanese boys, every day started and ended with guitars, an unparalleled trend seen in every corner of Japan.

However, in any age, there are adults who feel uncomfortable about the fashions of the young. The authorities decided that playing the electric guitar turned boys into delinquents. In October 1965, Ashikaga City Education Committee in Tochigi Prefecture issued a ban on electric guitars, instantly throwing cold water on the guitar boom. Schools followed suit, with rules banning electric guitars. Many public facilities became unavailable for hire if electric guitar playing was involved. Newspapers, which up until then had supported electric guitar competitions and reported them favourably, suddenly changed their attitude. They accused electric guitars of being a hotbed of evil. The electric guitar boom imploded. Of course, there is no knowing exactly how much pressure was imposed by the authorities, and we can't presume that this was the only reason the boom declined. But the fact is that the electric guitar boom waned and sales of each maker plummeted soon afterwards.

Another reason for this decline was that people had simply got bored with instrumental music. But in the background the Liverpool Sound, personified by The Beatles, was gaining

FIRSTMAN was one of the companies set up by ex-Teisco employees who left when Kawai bought Teisco. Firstman relied on the new popularity of The Beatles in Japan by using a *striking version of Höfner's "violin" body shape for the Liverpool 67 model. Its best-known player, Tunaki Mihara (right) of The Blue Comets, gave it valuable exposure.*

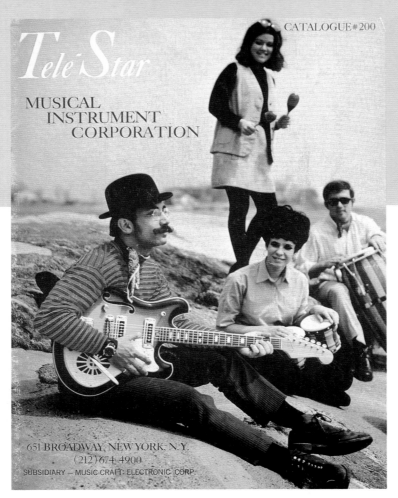

CATALOGUE #200

Tele Star

MUSICAL
INSTRUMENT
CORPORATION

651 BROADWAY, NEW YORK, N.Y.
(212) 674-4900
SUBSIDIARY — MUSIC-CRAFT ELECTRONIC CORP.

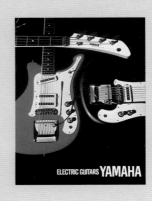

YAMAHA are one of the oldest Japanese music companies, with roots that go back to organ making in the 1880s. Observing the guitar boom of the 1960s, they decided to launch a solidbody line of electrics in 1966 (with this catalogue, left) bearing clear Fender and Mosrite influences.

JAPANESE guitar makers increasingly built instruments for export during the 1960s. Products of the bigger factories are seen with many different brands, often reflecting the marketing plans of the importer rather than the manufacturer's name. Telestar guitars (right) were made by Kawai in Japan, and the US importer has left us a document replete with such 1960s essentials as beehives, neckerchiefs and mini-skirts.

ground, and in June 1966 when The Beatles came to Japan their popularity got into full swing. Up until then the group's fans had mainly been girls, but now boys finally started to recognise The Beatles. Kids who had copied The Ventures by making instrumental music with solidbody guitars changed to vocal songs and hollow-body electric guitars, inspired by the Epiphones and Rickenbackers and Höfners they saw The Beatles playing. In 1966 many vocal groups — amateur and professional — made their debuts. The fashion was called Group Sounds, or 'GS' for short. The electric guitar boom had developed into the GS boom.

In 1967 and 1968 the GS boom swept Japan and with it sales of electric guitars increased again. Teisco had released the Framus-style V series hollow-body electric guitars. Solidbody guitars were unpopular, and so Teisco issued new models with a totally fresh design. These were the Spectrum 5 — which many consider the finest model produced by Teisco — and the tulip-shaped SM and K guitars (later taken up by

Humming Bird

OFFSET cutaways and a slanting pickup were taken straight from Mosrite for Tokai's Humming Bird, but translated into oriental style.

POP GROUPS blossomed in Japan, especially after The Beatles played at the Nippon Budokan Hall in Tokyo in summer 1966. The craze for making music that followed was called "Group Sounds", and everyone wanted to take part. Here are two examples: from the more obscure end, The Fingers (right), and the successful Sharp Five.

TOKYO SOUND CO was set up by Mitsuo Matsuki in the late 1940s to make Guyatone guitars (logo, below). With Teisco, Guyatone was the main Japanese electric guitar brand to have continued successfully into the 1960s from these early roots. The two benefitted from the initial rush of Ventures-inspired pop in Japan in 1965. Despite stronger competition during the Beatles-inspired "Group Sounds" fad of 1966, Guyatone scored by co-designing a guitar with Sharp Five's popular guitarist Nobuhiro Mine (left).

GUYATONE
TOKYO SOUND CO., LTD.

Jackson Browne/Ry Cooder collaborator David Lindley). The quality of these was far better than anything Teisco had produced before.

However, Teisco got into difficulties due to overstocking and a huge capital investment. In January 1967 they were taken over by Kawai Gakki, who began to produce Teisco guitars in their own factories. Under the umbrella of Kawai Gakki, Teisco released in 1968 a number of striking hollow-body electric models such as the May Queen, Vamper, Fire Bird and Phantom. In the uncertain period during the takeover of Teisco by Kawai, some disgruntled young engineers left Teisco to set up their own new companies, including Honey and Firstman.

Honey released a Rickenbacker copy, the SG-5, and this became a hit and made Honey almost instantly successful. Firstman released the unusual violin-shape Liverpool 67 model, as used by Tunaki Mihara, guitarist with The Blue Comets, who were at the peak of their popularity. It sold well and Firstman too became a well-known brand. Both companies began to unveil a stream of new hollow-body electric guitars (but, significantly, almost no solidbody models). If the stars of the 1965 boom were Teisco and Guyatone, it is no exaggeration to say that the heroes of the second boom were Honey and Firstman.

Another company born when Teisco was taken over by Kawai was Idol, established by a founder of Teisco, Doryu Matsuda, in September 1967. Matsuda had stayed on as a director of Kawai after the takeover, but left soon after to form Idol, which released only hollow-body electric guitars.

Guyatone too marketed a Rickenbacker-style hollow-body electric guitar, the SG-42T, as well as the solidbody LG-350T Sharp Five, jointly developed with Nobuhiro Mine who played guitar with the popular band Sharp Five.

In 1966 Yamaha entered the electric guitar market, with several solidbody models in the SG series and the hollow-body electric SA series. The latter were conspicuously high-quality models compared to other Japanese-made hollow-body electrics guitars of the period, and were taken up by a number of professionals. Arai was one of the companies which swiftly changed production from solid guitars to hollow-body electrics. In 1966 Aria's Gibson-style hollow-body electrics appeared. (Note that the company is called Arai but the brandname is Aria.)

Greco, who had until this time made instruments mainly for export, appeared on the domestic market in 1968 with Harmony-style hollow-body electric guitars. Around the same time Tokai – who would later take the world by storm with

▽ TOKAI HUMMING BIRD 200S
Produced 1968-1969; this example c1968

The Ventures instrumental group from the US enjoyed enormous popularity in Japan during the 1960s, mostly using Mosrite guitars in the process, and causing a near obsession among Japanese guitar makers with the look of the Mosrite Ventures model. This wonderful example shows how the American original was adapted to suit oriental tastes. In later decades Tokai would move to blatant copies of US designs, with notorious accuracy.

vintage replicas – entered the electric guitar market. They released Mosrite-influenced guitars under the Humming Bird brandname, the solidbody construction going against the contemporary trend. Manufacturing companies were springing up to take advantage of the demand and make money, and produced electric guitars with beautiful names but dubious identity, including brands such as Excetro, Jaguar, Liberty and Minister. One company even branded their guitars 'Burns', but with no connection at all to the UK operation.

As is so often the case, the boom didn't last long. In late 1968, GS started to decline and in '69 completely died out. The makers with excessive stocks went bankrupt – first Honey, then Firstman, followed by Idol and Guyatone (although Guyatone was later revived). By 1969 the domestic guitar industry in Japan was almost completely wiped out. It was the end of an era. Of course, some manufacturers such as Aria, Greco, Voice and Yamaha survived the crisis through sound management, and Teisco continued under the umbrella of Kawai Gakki. For these makers 1969 was a year of renewal. Greco turned its eyes to acoustic guitars and Gibson copies, and Aria tried to escape from the difficulties by joining the trend toward producing copies of classic US models. It would be these copy guitars that would dominate the Japanese guitar industry through much of the 1970s. ■ **HIROYUKI NOGUCHI**

◁ KUSTOM K200C
Produced 1968-1969; this example c1968

Meanwhile in Kansas, Kustom exemplified the small-scale American guitar maker trying to attract players away from big-name products. Despite designer Doyle Reading's experience gained at other modest operations such as Holman and Alray, Kustom had nothing special enough to commend its guitars, and would enter the 1970s as solely an amplifier manufacturer.

1968

MICRO-FRETS was set up by Ralph Jones (right, with The Orbiter – and his wife Hazel – at a trade show in 1968). As well as the first wireless guitar, Micro-Frets offered a number of other models, some with the complex Calibrato vibrato system and the 'Micro-Nut', intended to stabilise tuning and improve intonation. The inventive, stylish Micro-Frets guitars did not, however, last long into the next decade.

THE ORBITER had an FM radio transmitter built into the body: the antenna can be seen on its upper horn (above). A remote receiver then picked up the signals and directed them to the player's stage amplifier.

BLUES & SOUL GUITARS

The electric guitar had become the key instrument in black American music, with the lead guitarist vying for the dominant role. Yet over the decade a fundamental change took place. In black music the electric guitar was absorbed back into a more anonymous role in the band, while during the same period a new generation of English interpreters performed the converse move, making the lead guitarist arguably the most significant force in mainstream popular music.

By 1960 the electric guitar had irrevocably changed the format of R&B. At the beginning of the 1950s, the saxophone and brass section had formed the mainstay of black music, but in a single decade they had been almost completely supplanted by small combos based around the electric guitar.

Blues music had reached an impressive state of technical sophistication. In Chicago, the capital city of electric blues, the Vee Jay and Chess record companies had enjoyed a cosy duopoly, with a definitive roster of acts including Muddy Waters, Howlin' Wolf and Jimmy Reed. However, by the late

1950s, a new generation of guitarists had appeared in the city. Buddy Guy, Otis Rush and Magic Sam – all of whom made their initial impact via the shortlived Cobra label based on Chicago's West Side – were heavily influenced by B.B. King, and along with fellow newcomer Freddy King helped establish the lead guitarist as the central figure in electric bands. Their guitar-dominated music was termed West Side blues, although as Buddy Guy points out "that word is just a label, 'cause we all played the same clubs, West Side, South Side, whatever".

Although the flowering of West Side blues was brief, it left a legacy of influential records which demonstrated how the music had developed to a form that anticipated the blues-rock of the end of the decade. Guy, Rush and 'Magic' Sam Maghett all used Fender Stratocasters amplified through Fender's beefy 4x10 Bassman combo – an amplifier designed, as its name suggests, for bass, but which was perfectly suited for powerful overdriven lead guitar sounds. Freddy King used a Gibson Les Paul gold-top or an ES-335, reportedly through a Dual Showman stack. In every case the trademark sound of these players hinged on the sustain and responsiveness of their solidbody (or semi-solid) electric guitars.

It's often remarked that the key solidbody electrics were

OTIS RUSH exemplified the West Side cocktail of blues and soul, but his career was dogged by ill-fortune. This 1969 LP, Mourning In The Morning, produced by Mike Bloomfield, occupied similar ground to Albert King's Born Under A Bad Sign, but was released too late to enjoy similar success.

PLAYERS *such as Eric Clapton and Peter Green had spearheaded a British blues-rock movement that relied heavily on the 1950s-style version of Gibson's Les Paul guitars, particularly the* Sunburst. *Gibson reissued a couple of models (but not the Sunburst) in 1968. As their launch ad from that year (right) admitted: "The pressure to make more has never let up. Okay... you win."*

Daddy of 'em all.

Gibson Guitars and Amps.

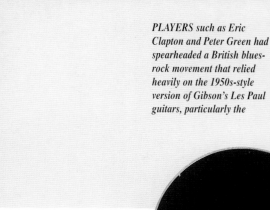

△ GIBSON LES PAUL CUSTOM

Produced 1968-current (this style); this example c1969

Even Gibson noticed the enormous interest in old-design Les Pauls during the second half of the 1960s, but in 1968 reissued the Custom and the gold-top rather than the revered Sunburst.

The Orbiter

△ MICRO-FRETS THE ORBITER

Produced 1968-1969; this example c1968

Today it's commonplace to see guitars and microphones linked from the live stage by wireless transmitters, but this innovative instrument – made by the Micro-Frets company of Maryland – was the first wireless guitar, well ahead of its time.

Micro-Frets

CORPORATION OF   FREDERICK, MARYLAND

invented by Fender or Gibson, and then reinvented by Hendrix and Clapton. But the recorded legacy of West Side blues, as well as earlier records by B.B. King, Guitar Slim and others, demonstrated that these players had developed an equally profound understanding of the electric guitar's potential. Their influence on some of the city's elder bluesmen was substantial, too. Muddy Waters drew on the services of Buddy Guy, while Howlin' Wolf, in conjunction with Chess writing mainstay Willie Dixon, recruited both Guy and Freddy King for studio duties, alongside Wolf's favoured lead guitarist Hubert Sumlin. This ensured that Howlin' Wolf enjoyed hits well into the 1960s, and according to many local commentators helped him retain a far bigger fan-base than his long-term rival, Muddy Waters.

Although the West Side bluesmen were responsible for a final flowering of the blues single, prompted in part by a realisation that the heyday of American blues was ending, artists such as Clyde McPhatter, Ray Charles and Sam Cooke had started incorporating gospel elements into their music back in the 1950s. By 1961 the commercial success of soul music was overshadowing the blues.

In many cases the difference between blues and soul was simply a question of marketing – most of the West Side bluesmen incorporated soul songs into their set, while Sam Cooke covered Willie Dixon's 'Little Red Rooster'. But the market for traditional bluesmen such as Muddy Waters and Jimmy Reed soon dried up outside their heartland in Chicago and the South.

In turn, blues labels such as Chess and Duke turned to a new generation of soul-blues performers, including Little

BUDDY GUY (left) was one of the key guitarists in the blossoming of 1960s Chicago blues, nicknamed West Side for the area of the city in which it developed. The tough, stinging Strat was the guitar of choice for many of the West Siders, as Guy, who began using Fenders in 1958, recently explained to Dan Erlewine. "I was always a wild man with the guitar, and a lot of times when you play like that the guitar has to be rough," he said. "So I went for the Strat, and I've had it fly off the top of a car going 80 miles an hour in Africa. The case bust open, it fell out, and there wasn't but one key out of tune." Magic Sam was another West Side bluesman, and this impressive 1968 album (left) has become a classic. Only a year later he was dead at 32.

71

1969

ROSEWOOD Telecasters were rarely seen, but an important sighting of the guitar did occur when George Harrison played one on The Beatles' famous Apple rooftop 'concert' in 1969.

▷ **FENDER ROSEWOOD TELECASTER**
Produced 1969-1972; this example c1969

Here was an unusual variant on Fender's enduring Telecaster design: this model had a body made entirely from heavy rosewood. Guitarists would of course be familiar with the wood from guitar fingerboards, but rosewood had rarely been used for a relatively large solid body – and apparently, when one picked up a Rosewood Telecaster, with good reason. Fender became aware of the obvious criticism quite quickly, and later versions of the rosewood Tele employed a modified body that had two separate pieces for front and back, and hollowed chambers within, all designed to ease the load on the player's shoulder.

GIBSON's Personal has a mike socket (right) on the body edge, another odd idea of Les Paul's.

▽ **GIBSON LES PAUL PERSONAL**
Produced 1969-1972; this example c1969

With guitarist Les Paul back in an advisory role at Gibson following the re-introduction of the original 1950s designs, the company indulged the great man's passion for low-impedance pickups with the Professional model and this Personal which, as the name implies, was based on Les Paul's own instrument.

MUDDY WATERS was a star in the 1960s. "I do the same thing for white audiences that I do for black," he said. "I get down and do real blues."

Milton Campbell and fellow Memphis singer Bobby Bland (whose outfit included the inspired lead guitarist Wayne Bennett). But their modest success on the R&B charts was eclipsed by the output of hit-oriented labels such as Motown. The Detroit company's records were masterful mini pop symphonies, but their tight musical choreography left little room for the electric guitar – if anything, the bass guitar took on more prominence, thanks to champions like James Jamerson whose imaginative basslines powered Motown hits such as The Supremes' 'You Keep Me Hangin' On'.

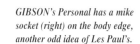

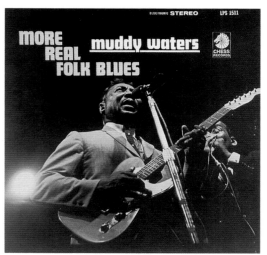

Although the role of the blues lead guitar player was becoming less prominent into the 1960s, there was no shortage of talented guitarists contributing to American R&B

hits. As well as writer/producers such as Curtis Mayfield, key soul players included Marv Tarplin, who contributed gorgeously melodic guitar to Smokey Robinson's 'You Really Got A Hold On Me' and 'The Tracks Of My Tears'. Also notable were Bobby Womack, and Robert Ward, who developed a distinctive guitar style based on subtle two-note runs and the signature vibrato sound of the Magnavox amp.

Ward played guitar on Wilson Pickett's first hit, The Falcons' 'I Found A Love', and exemplified the move to a grittier, funkier style of guitar playing. Like contemporaries such as Redding and Pickett, Ward had grown up in a musically eclectic radio-dominated environment. "I listened to Sam Cooke and the Soul Stirrers, Five Blind Boys, and the Nightingales," he says. "I listened to a lot of Jimmy Reed, Muddy Waters, and John Lee Hooker. And I played country and Western, Hank Williams and Roy Rogers. Then I tried to play all of that at once, and no

FENDER increasingly gave the impression as the 1960s drew to a close that it had lost its way. The CBS-owned operation even took to botching together a guitar called the Custom (seen at the bottom of this Fender ad from 1969) out of parts left over from obsolete models... and then had the cheek to announce that "it's new, from head to strap button".

WOODSTOCK in upstate New York hosts 400,000 music lovers cast in a sea of mud and entertained by Jimi Hendrix, Sly & The Family Stone, Richie Havens, Crosby Stills Nash & Young, Santana, Joe Cocker, The Who, Ten Years After and others.

I couldn't... but I did the best I could." Blues music had always been influenced by country. Performers like Lowell Fulson or B.B. King had namechecked Western Swing bands such as Bob Wills' back in the 1950s. By the early 1960s the influence of country rhythm playing – alternating bottom-string bass notes with clipped chords, or using the two-note Memphis scale – was becoming more and more apparent in soul guitar playing. And apart from the black players who were checking out country music, a new generation of white players had been listening carefully to Jimmy Reed or Elmore James. Before long this would create an ironic situation, with black Motown musicians making hit records largely for white audiences, while a new crop of white musicians contributed to hits largely for a black clientele.

Back in the 1950s, Elvis Presley had tapped into the gloriously rich musical culture of the American South to make some of the most iconoclastic records of his era. His stint with the US army brought his influence to a premature end, but there were other musicians who, like Elvis, had been imbued with the blues music that permeated the cities. Atlantic producer Jerry Wexler was among the first to notice the significance of this development when he started licensing records from Jim Stewart and Estelle Axton of the Stax label. These Memphis partners had built a primitive studio in an old cinema, the home of the most celebrated studio band in popular music: the MGs. A racially integrated outfit led by organist Booker T, with Steve Cropper on guitar, the MGs cut the hugely successful 'Green Onions' under their own name, and contributed to countless hits by Otis Redding, Sam & Dave, Wilson Pickett and others.

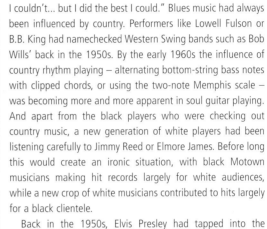

Steve Cropper's distinctive style – brittle, precise rhythmic chops and vicious, stabbing solos wrenched out of a 1950s Telecaster – retained all of the emotion of classic blues guitar but packaged into short, single-friendly bursts. Cropper's style was totally distinct from that of someone like Robert Ward, for example, but was nonetheless a similarly powerful example of how classic soul guitar playing relied as much on the injection of country-type styles into blues as it did on the more generally accepted influence of gospel.

As Etta James, who would go on to record in Muscle Shoals, puts it, "A lot of that Otis Redding stuff is country to me. 'I've Been Loving You Too Long' for instance is a pure country

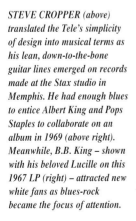

STEVE CROPPER (above) translated the Tele's simplicity of design into musical terms as his lean, down-to-the-bone guitar lines emerged on records made at the Stax studio in Memphis. He had enough blues to entice Albert King and Pops Staples to collaborate on an album in 1969 (above right). Meanwhile, B.B. King – shown with his beloved Lucille on this 1967 LP (right) – attracted new white fans as blues-rock became the focus of attention.

AMPEG offered the Dan Armstrong See Through guitar (ad, left) with six slide-in/slide-out pickups: Rock, Country and Jazz, with a Treble and Bass variety of each. Two were supplied with the guitar; the others were available from dealers. If the "revolutionary" plastic body became scratched, Ampeg suggested buffing with a dollop of hi-tech toothpaste.

DAN ARMSTRONG · AMPEG

song." But Pops Staples – whose gospel guitar work with The Staple Singers would influence the sound of soul – points out, "Putting categories on those things is tricky. I called our music gospel with a blues kick, myself, but people would say to me, 'What would you call that, country?'"

The success of the MGs paved the way for several other outfits, including the Muscle Shoals studio band, with Spooner Oldham on keyboards and guitarists Eddie Hinton and Jimmy Johnson, the Hi Records house band, overseen by producer Willie Mitchell, and the American house band, established by Chips Moman. Each band featured the democratic arrangement of the Stax outfit, emphasising the new role of the electric guitar: subordinated to the song and to the rhythm. Previously there had been many blues lead guitarists – B.B. King the most prominent - who professed little interest in rhythm guitar. By the 1960s, good rhythm chops were just about the most vital qualifications on an aspiring R&B guitarist's CV.

Several performers were vying for the leadership of soul music through the mid 1960s. In 1965 James Brown achieved almost undisputed command of the title with his masterstroke,

'Papa's Got A Brand New Bag'. Brown had established a rigid format for his trademark sound, based on 'the one'. This meant hitting the first beat of a two-bar pattern in unison, then basing the rhythm on the off-beat for the rest of the phrase. On 'Bag', Brown finally found a guitarist who could inhabit this new rhythmic world. Jimmy Nolen, previously a straight blues player, had become fascinated by the complex rhythms of Bo Diddley songs. Diddley describes his own sound as deriving from his inability to play like Muddy Waters or John Lee Hooker. Instead, his distinctive style came from "playing on the guitar exactly what they play on drums".

Modifying Diddley's scratchy rhythms, and simplifying his parts to fit in with Maceo Parker's intricate horn arrangement, Nolen came up with what would soon be titled funk guitar. It was a powerful reminder that, despite being unfashionable as a lead instrument, the electric guitar would never be consigned to a completely anonymous role within the rhythm section. And of course, even as Brown recorded some of his greatest songs, white guitarists on the other side of the Atlantic were in the process of recreating the electric guitar as the ultimate lead instrument.

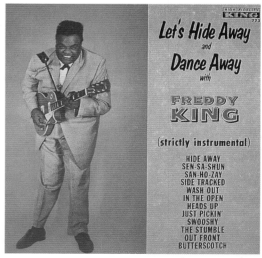

Let's Hide Away and Dance Away with FREDDY KING

(strictly instrumental)

HIDE AWAY
SEN-SA-SHUN
SAN-HO-ZAY
SIDE TRACKED
WASH OUT
IN THE OPEN
HEADS UP
JUST PICKIN'
SWOOSHY
THE STUMBLE
OUT FRONT
BUTTERSCOTCH

FREDDY KING recorded in the late 1950s and early 1960s some classic guitar-soaked

blues cuts, an influential batch of which appeared on this album (above) in 1961.

△ AMPEG DAN ARMSTRONG "BLACK"
Produced 1969; this example 1969

*A small number, possibly only eight, of the Dan Amstrong model
were made with a black plastic body rather than the usual clear
material. It has been suggested that these rare guitars may
have been produced as promotional items for instrument retailers.*

△ AMPEG DAN ARMSTRONG "SEE-THROUGH"
Produced 1969-1970; this example c1969

*Ampeg had been started by Everett Hull in New York in the late
1940s, making amps and bass pickups. By 1968 a new direction
was sought, and local guitar repairman Dan Armstrong was hired
to design a new line of guitars. Armstrong decided to carve
bodies from blocks of clear perspex, intending to make the result
distinctive as much as to exploit the sonic potential of the
material. But the imaginative "See Through" and its matching
bass lasted little more than a year in production, hindered by
conservative players and an expensive manufacturing process.*

*ERIC CLAPTON defined
British blues-rock guitar
playing when in 1966 he made
Blues Breakers (right) with
John Mayall. Even those who
had not seen the band live were
intrigued by the picture on the
back of the sleeve (inset, right)
of Clapton with a Les Paul
Sunburst. The instrument
became the aim for many a
spotty white kid who suddenly
had the blues. Clapton himself
had decided on a Les Paul
when he saw Freddy King with
one on his Dance Away album
(left). King actually had a gold-
top, but Clapton thought it was
a Sunburst. This mistaken
identity led the 1958-1960
Gibson Les Paul Sunburst to
become the most collectible
solidbody guitar ever made.*

For many observers, the British blues boom started on the
day that Eric Clapton came in to replace the under-age Top
Topham in The Yardbirds. Topham was a competent musician,
but Clapton's arrival put the band into a whole new musical
league. For the habitués of London's Crawdaddy Club, the
band's regular haunt after The Rolling Stones gave up their
residency, Clapton's playing was a revelation. Topham puts
Clapton's success down to "what Eric was listening to. The
only blues we'd heard was Muddy Waters or John Lee Hooker,
but Eric had access to the really hot stuff – Freddy King records
that people like [DJ] Guy Stevens brought in. Eric would come
out with licks no one could believe, then later on I found out
that a lot of it came straight from those Freddy King records."

Freddy King's influence permeates Clapton's early work, but
although he'd learned the guitarist's trademark riffs, Clapton's
greatest achievement was his mastery of Freddy's musical
aggression. As Mike Vernon, who produced Clapton in his phase
with John Mayall's Bluesbreakers, points out, "Eric's playing was
a revelation at the time. In England no one had heard that
aggression, that commitment and grittiness." Crucially, Clapton

and now !

BASSES

and

GUITARS

by *Ampeg*

△ DAN ARMSTRONG MODIFIED DANELECTRO
Produced 1969; this example 1969

When MCA closed Danelectro at the end of the 1960s, Dan Armstrong bought some old stock. This guitar is one of the results: a 1950s-style Danelectro body/neck with a humbucking pickup and suitable pickguard inscription. Some were sold through Ampeg, others over the counter at Armstrong's store.

also unleashed the potential of the Gibson Les Paul – which he'd bought after seeing a photo of King with one on the cover of his *Hide Away* album – and combined it with the Marshall amplifiers that had started to become popular early in 1965. Overdriving his Marshall model-1962 combo with his Les Paul Sunburst's humbucking pickups, Clapton created a sound which would become the mainstay of late-1960s rock.

In Clapton's wake many English guitarists would harness the sounds created by American blues guitarists almost a decade before. In the US Mike Bloomfield and others would master blues techniques and help kick off the psychedelic rock boom, while the country's original bluesmen would enjoy a career revival thanks to the late-1960s blues boom.

Yet it would be an American who would complete the development of late-1960s rock guitar, by adding mid-1960s R&B styles to the rock guitarist's tonal palette. Jimi Hendrix, a master of both the authentic delta blues of Muddy Waters and the rhythm guitar of Curtis Mayfield or Steve Cropper, introduced innumerable innovations to rock guitar and ensured that blues lead guitar styles finally crossed over to the mainstream. Many observers commented that Hendrix's first-hand blues knowledge and black culture gave him a crucial advantage over England's blue-eyed bluesmen. What most failed to observe was that Jimi's acquaintance with soul rhythm-guitar styles meant he wasn't just bringing so-called black elements into rock guitar. For as his producer, Chas Chandler, commented to this writer, "One thing I would point out about his playing was how much country there was in it. All those little rhythmic and chordal fills are classic country guitar. As a blues lead guitarist he could play his rivals into the ground, and I saw him do it. But the reason his songs worked, to me, was because of the way he understood country guitar playing." ∎ PAUL TRYNKA

JIMMY NOLEN (above, right) played the machine-like rhythm guitar on many of James Brown's funk masterworks. Nolen joined Brown in 1965 for 'Papa's Got A Brand New Bag' and helped build awesome grooves like 'Licking Stick' and 'Mother Popcorn', staying in the band until he died in 1983.

JIMI HENDRIX boasted a quintessential 1960s mix of blues and soul – more than enough to inspire hundreds of memorable live shows, a string of biting singles and three superb albums, combining to

fill his tragically short career to bursting point. Something had to give. Jimi told Melody Maker in 1969: "People see a fast buck and have you up there being a slave to the public. They keep you at it until you are exhausted, and so is the public, and then they move off to other things. That's why groups break up – they just get worn out. Musicians want to pull away after a while, or they get lost in the whirlpool." Jimi died in 1970, just 27 years old.

BOB B. SOXX & THE BLUE JEANS 'Zip-A-Dee-Do-Dah' A-side 1962; Billy Strange
"To make a live mix, the engineer turned all 12 of the mixer's rotary volume controls off, then brought them in one by one. When he got to 11, Phil Spector said to stop. The guitar mike stayed off, but (somewhat symbolically of things to come) enough guitar sound spilled around to come through the other mikes." JOHN MORRISH

PHIL SPECTOR teaches two studio hands the chords to another little symphony.

20, he took his group out of his record company's own studios and insisted on recording them elsewhere. The Beach Boy then promptly took control of the whole artistic process, even leaving the touring band to concentrate on maintaining their punishing schedule of record releases.

Soon his favourite studios would be block-booked for weeks at a time. As he began to work with orchestral musicians and the cream of the Los Angeles session scene, laying down the tracks to which his fellow Beach Boys would later add vocals, Wilson found the studio a congenial place to write, arrange and hang out. 'Good Vibrations' was among the first recordings to be made in this way. "I tried to make a pocket symphony out of this record," Wilson told Don Traynor in 1966. In effect it is a composition for recording studio – four were used – completed over six months in 1966 at a cost of more than $50,000. The contrast with the experience of The Shadows, only a few years earlier, could not be more marked.

THE VENTURES 'Lullaby Of The Leaves' A-side 1961; Bob Bogle (lead, Fender Stratocaster) with Don Wilson
"This blasts out of the chute with a 'Walk – Don't Run' style intro and then kicks into an ascending melody that's topped off with a radical (for the time) whammy dip. One of the first hit instrumentals in which the whammy was integral to the melody, it also has a driving bass/guitar/drums unison 16th-note chorus." TOM WHEELER

But Wilson, like many artists in the coming months, discovered he liked this way of working. He told Traynor: "The stimulation I get from moulding music and from adding dynamics is like nothing else on earth. If you take the *Pet Sounds* album as a collection of art pieces, each designed to stand alone yet which belong together, you'll see what I was aiming at. I sat up in my house for five months, planning every stage of the album. I have a big Spanish table, circular, and I sit there hour after hour making the tunes inside my head. I love peaks in a song, and enhancing them on the control panel. I get such a kick out of bending electricity and recording techniques to make them work for us. They're there to be used, maximum. Top maximum." Wilson now planned a whole album made up of fragments – composed, arranged and recorded in the studio. Masses of music was recorded and dubbed on to acetate discs to allow Wilson to come up with some sort of sequence. In the event, *Smile*, as it was intended to be known, collapsed in ruins as Wilson's artistic control and self-confidence imploded.

One of the factors in Brian Wilson's decline was the imminent arrival of The Beatles' *Sgt Pepper's Lonely Hearts Club Band*, released in June 1967, a month after he had scrapped the *Smile* project. The Beatles had, if anything, been slightly behind Wilson in their artistic adventurousness up to that point. Now they took the lead. Paradoxically, it was as representatives of an unsophisticated, street-level musical consciousness far removed from anything elaborate that The Beatles had first appealed to George Martin, the unorthodox

EMI A&R man – his background was in comedy records – who was to become their producer and studio mentor.

Their first singles and their first album were done rapidly on a two-track machine, vocals on one track and instruments on the other, and the only complication was in getting an acceptable sound from the group's rather poor guitars, drums and amps. At their initial session, for instance, someone had to cobble together a monitoring amp plus a speaker from the echo chamber to make Paul McCartney a usable bass amp.

Later, though, the in-house engineering expertise of Abbey Road was to become invaluable as The Beatles began to experiment in ways that were not dependent upon mere musical expertise. Braving the wrath of EMI (written permission was required to put a microphone within 18" of a bass drum), Abbey Road engineers like Geoff Emerick began experimenting with close-miking. Later The Beatles, under the influence of either Musique Concrete, LSD or The Goons, wanted to use multiple tape loops in the recording of 'Tomorrow Never Knows'. At Abbey Road, there were always plenty of people around who knew how to do things like that.

BOOKER T & THE MGs
'Green Onions' A-side 1962;
Steve Cropper (Fender
Telecaster)
"Steve Cropper's stinging, string-torturing licks hit so hard that he only needed to launch them in the sparsest of clusters. In F, of all keys, and at the tender age of 20, Cropper wielded his stock Telecaster to devastating effect in this classic R&B instrumental."
TOMMY GOLDSMITH
"If one extreme of 1960s guitar was prolix, effects-laden and overdriven, the other was bright, tight-lipped and burnished. Memphis mofo Steve Cropper here delivered the ultimate in lean, mean and clean: elegant, understated Telecaster classicism that didn't waste a single pickstroke. Clint Eastwood was like a hysterical blabbermouth in comparison."
CHARLES SHAAR MURRAY

WES MONTGOMERY 'West
Coast Blues' from "Movin'
Wes" LP 1964; Wes
Montgomery (Gibson L5-CES)
"Purists tend to consider Montgomery's Riverside recordings as his best, but I remember being more thrilled then by Verve LPs like Movin' Wes or Smokin' At The Half Note. The power and the swing that emanate from this shorter version of his most popular composition is incredible – and his rendition of 'Caravan' on the same LP is well worth a listen, too." ANDRÉ DUCHOSSOIR

THE VENTURES 'Slaughter
On Tenth Avenue' A-side
1964; Nokie Edwards (lead,
Mosrite Ventures), plus Don
Wilson
"For me this is the best example of the playing of Nokie Edwards on a Ventures track, and I much prefer this to The Shadows' version. Originally bassist with the group, Edwards had swapped instrumental roles with guitarist Bob Bogle in 1963. There is a wonderful sound to Edwards' guitar on this track, where almost every guitar technique is included. This is how I was taught that lead guitar should be played."
HIROYUKI NOGUCHI

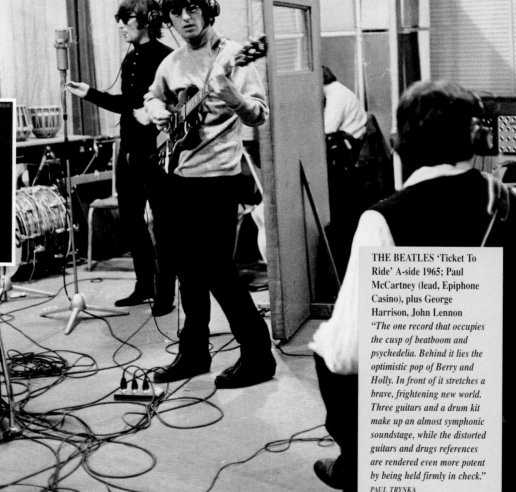

THE BEATLES 'Ticket To
Ride' A-side 1965; Paul
McCartney (lead, Epiphone
Casino), plus George
Harrison, John Lennon
"The one record that occupies the cusp of beatboom and psychedelia. Behind it lies the optimistic pop of Berry and Holly. In front of it stretches a brave, frightening new world. Three guitars and a drum kit make up an almost symphonic soundstage, while the distorted guitars and drugs references are rendered even more potent by being held firmly in check."
PAUL TRYNKA

THE BEATLES working on
'Paperback Writer' in EMI's
No.2 studio, April 1966.

THE REMO FOUR 'Peter Gunn' B-side 1964; Colin Manley (Fender Jazzmaster)
"This was an impressive British all-guitar version of Duane Eddy's hit, with the sax lead lines accurately re-created by Manley ("He makes most other British guitarists sound old-fashioned," said George Harrison in 1964). Keith Moon-style manic drumming contributed to an over-the-top performance which made me realise that guitar playing shouldn't be taken too seriously." PAUL DAY

ROY ORBISON 'Oh Pretty Woman' A-side 1964; Jerry Kennedy (lead, Gibson ES-335), plus Wayne Moss and Billy Sanford
"The signature lick is everything – melody, rhythm, chord structure and, most important, attitude. Orbison wrote the lick but on the session he played rhythm on a Gibson acoustic 12-string. The record was a line of demarcation, ending an era of thin, lyrical lead guitar styles and establishing the new, aggressive, in-your-face style that led to 'Satisfaction', 'Day Tripper' and all that followed." WALTER CARTER

THE BEACH BOYS 'Fun, Fun, Fun' A-side 1964; Carl Wilson (Fender Jaguar)
"I'm not sure I'd even heard of Chuck Berry when I first heard this record, but the arresting 17-second intro, borrowed from Berry's 'Back In The USA', has always epitomised rock'n'roll guitar to me. Carl Wilson was 17 at the time. He's been plagued ever since by people wanting reassurance that yes, he really did play it." JOHN MORRISH

THE BEACH BOYS recording Pet Sounds in 1966 (this page). Producer, artistic director and genius Brian Wilson is in the suitably artful spectacles.

Rewiring the rotating-speaker Leslie cabinet of the studio organ so that Lennon could sing through it, on the same song, was a matter of a few minutes. Invited to indulge their creativity, too, the Abbey Road engineers came up with a string of electronic inventions, most of them built around the idea of taking sound from the tape machine's 'sync' output (using the recording head to play back) and mixing it, after a suitable delay, with the normal playback output. The first was ADT (artificial double-tracking), designed to save Lennon the trouble of singing everything twice. That led directly to 'flanging' and 'STEED' (Send Tape Echo Echo Delay), a flutter-echo vocal effect showcased on 'A Day In The Life'.

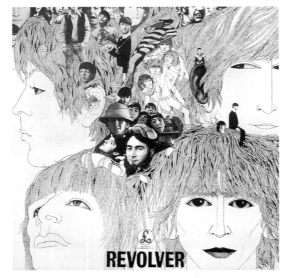

Although most of *Sgt Pepper's* was recorded on four-track ('A Day In The Life' being the famous exception, using two four-track machines linked up to provide seven tracks), The Beatles were eager to exploit new resources as they became available. When they found that, inexplicably, Abbey Road was booked when they wanted to record 'Hey Jude' in 1968 they went to Trident studios and found what was then one of a very few working eight-track recorders in London.

However, returning to Abbey Road they discovered that EMI had an eight-track machine in the laboratory being

THE BEATLES 'And Your Bird Can Sing' from "Revolver" LP 1966; George Harrison (lead, Gibson SG Standard), plus John Lennon or Paul McCartney
"Someone once called this 'the best guitar playing you ever heard' and I'd be hard put to disagree. George, along with harmonies by John or Paul (memories differ), provides an ultra-bright, 16th-note rampage as intro, backing and riveting solo for the proto-hippie tune. As well as Revolver, check out the Anthology 2 version for a more Byrds-influenced take, complete with Rick 12-string." TOMMY GOLDSMITH
"In my view, the combination of George Harrison and John Lennon is one of the best in the whole of 1960s guitar playing, and on this track you can hear elaborate guitar licks and an emotional harmony at work. Listen too for the way in which the twin guitar phrasing is deployed with such a mastery of melody." HIROYUKI NOGUCHI

Clapton was to find solace at various points in his career in a different Anglo-American tradition, one of self-conscious simplicity and authenticity rather than artistic contrivance. This was not simply a matter of taking inspiration from black music – the production-line soul of Motown was as painstakingly crafted as anything by The Beatles or Phil Spector – but of black music that consciously adhered to the blues tradition. The recordings produced for Atlantic and Stax by Tom Dowd were notable for their concentration on basic musical interplay – 'feel' – rather than arrangement or tricky engineering.

Certainly Dowd used the best equipment he could get. Atlantic's New York studios were among the first anywhere to have eight-track, which had been used by producers Leiber & Stoller to create hits for The Coasters and The Drifters since the late 1950s. But Dowd insisted on the simplest of engineering: one microphone per channel, wherever possible, and no equalisation (tonal adjustment) on the desk. When Dowd went to the Stax studios, a converted 500-seat cinema in Memphis, Tennessee, things were even more basic. Recording was done straight to mono, with a minimum of microphones. A five-piece horn section might have two microphones on them, which would require them to balance themselves. But such musical skills were readily available.

In 1967, Eric Clapton's Cream came to Atlantic studios and Dowd recorded their *Disraeli Gears* album on eight-track. After initial dismay at the sheer volume produced by the three-piece, Dowd settled down and made the album in three days. This combination of musical virtuosity and engineering simplicity offered a different route to that explored by The Beatles in the latter part of the 1960s, where the sophistication was in arrangement and engineering. This was a tussle that was to be

THE BUTTERFIELD BLUES BAND 'East-West' from "East-West" LP 1966; Mike Bloomfield and Elvin Bishop (Bloomfield Gibson Les Paul gold-top; Bishop probably Gibson ES-335)
"In this sprawling 13-minute instrumental rock raga Bloomfield and Bishop intertwined modal melodies in pulsed crescendos punctuated by Butterfield's brilliant harp. It's one of the earliest flings in 1960s pop culture's emerging affair with eastern philosophy and psychedelia, creating the model for the twin-lead heavy guitar rock that was to follow." MICHAEL WRIGHT

'evaluated'. So they persuaded engineer Dave Harries to let them use it on 'While My Guitar Gently Weeps', a piece also notable for the fact that Eric Clapton's guest guitar, rather than the vocal, is put through the ADT machine. This single song took some 37 hours to record, approximately 37 times as long as the average Shadows number of a few years earlier. The Beatles were self-evidently falling apart during the making of *'The White Album'*, and subsequent efforts did nothing to slow this decline. The recording process as it had developed in the mid 1960s was often destructive of bands and their creativity. An extremely boring process for those not actually laying down tracks, it magnified minor technical failings and brought 'artistic differences' to the fore. Eric Clapton famously left The Yardbirds because a harpsichord was dropped into their 1964 single 'For Your Love'. "Where does that leave me?" he complained. "Twelve-string guitar, I suppose."

CREAM 'Sunshine Of Your Love' from "Disraeli Gears" LP 1967; Eric Clapton (Gibson SG Standard)
"The song and the riff are true classics from the late 1960s and form a timeless vehicle for improvisation. But 'Sunshine Of Your Love' also exemplifies Clapton's typical 'woman tone' which many aspiring guitarists were then keen to imitate. It looked even better when played live and loud on a painted SG Standard." ANDRÉ DUCHOSSOIR

played out again and again during the next decade. Multitrack recording – 16-track was introduced towards the end of the 1960s – had made it possible for those with no musical vision and limited instrumental expertise to produce complex-sounding music by the simple process of adding and subtracting until they found something that worked. This was entirely new. Previously, composers and arrangers had always needed a sound in their heads before they started. In the 1960s, musicians and record producers – who were increasingly enjoying 'auteur' status akin to that enjoyed by contemporary film directors – were freed from that requirement. The stage was set both for a new type of creativity and an epic era of self-indulgence.

In both respects, Jimi Hendrix showed himself to be at the forefront. He had made recordings throughout his career, right back to his days on the 'chitlin circuit', the black music clubs of America. In 1967 he took the Experience into Olympic Studios in London for the first sessions with engineer Eddie Kramer. "Basically," explained Kramer, in a 1992 article for *EQ* magazine, "he created the sound in the amp and I just took it and ran with it – expanded upon it." Hendrix's sound came from a few favourite pedals, overdriven amplifiers and his own hands. Kramer helped where he could, for instance by creating stereo phasing to give him "an underwater sound he had

heard in his dreams". For vocal recording, which Hendrix loathed, he put him behind screens and kept the lights dim. This womb-like ambience was to be central to Electric Lady, Hendix's own studio in New York. Musicians had had their own studios before, but this was to be the real thing, with the first true 24-track mixer and tape machine.

Hendrix's dream was to be able to record day or night, for as long as he wanted. But Electric Lady also represented a sanctuary, a safe haven for a man who had always had a problem with the word "No". In particular, it allowed him to escape his touring self, a psychedelic showman for whom music came a poor second.

Electric Lady opened in the summer of 1970. Hendrix recorded some tracks for *Rainbow Bridge* there, but it was too late. He died in September of that year. But this new use for the recording studio, as a sympathetic artistic refuge in a hostile world, was to become common in the years ahead. ■ JOHN MORRISH

THE YARDBIRDS 'Shapes Of Things' single A-side 1966; Jeff Beck (lead, Fender Esquire), plus Chris Dreja
"I was 13 years old, my first guitar still a good nine months into the future. Across the fuzzy ether from Wonderful Radio London came what sounded like an alien marching tune, interrupted by the most demented, far-out musical noise my young ears had heard. Was that a guitar? It must have been – each time it came on I would leap to my feet, hands convulsing Cocker-like in ludicrous imitation of its crazy execution. It was going to be a fantastic year." DAVE GREGORY

JIMI HENDRIX EXPERIENCE 'Are You Experienced' from "Are You Experienced" LP 1967; Jimi Hendrix (Fender Stratocaster)
"As a mature 14-year-old I'd already learned to play all the songs off From Nowhere... The Troggs. So Jimi's debut album came as a bit of a shock. After 35 minutes of the music of the gods, Hendrix closed the record with this stunning track, apparently created almost entirely in reverse. It was remarkable that anything musical could be achieved from such a random process, yet here was an emotional, coherent, perfectly-executed solo that I am still unable to turn away from whenever I hear it. Who but Hendrix would have dared attempt such a feat and pull it off so perfectly?" DAVE GREGORY

JIMI HENDRIX ready to rock with Strat, Vox wah and Fuzz Face at TTG studio in 1968.

STEPPENWOLF 'Magic Carpet Ride' A-side 1968; Michael Monarch (lead, Fender Esquire), plus John Kay
"It's the rhythm. While most guitarists were concentrating on the blues, Steppenwolf followed the example of the early rockers and took the rhythm element from R&B. They kicked it into overdrive and came up with a crunching rhythm sound so strong that a conventional lead part was unnecessary." WALTER CARTER

TONY WILLIAMS LIFETIME 'Spectrum' from "Emergency" LP 1969; John McLaughlin (Gibson Les Paul Custom)
"Tipped from the mid 1960s as a guitarist to watch, McLaughlin confirmed his arrival as a major innovative force with the playing on this track. Its angular theme, crunchy chords, soaring melody and urgent rock rhythms springboard McLaughlin into a blistering solo of Hendrix-like intensity, the fresh harmonic ideas and technical fluency of which announce the agenda for the jazz-rock and fusion music that was to come in the 1970s." CHARLES ALEXANDER

83

INDEX

Song titles are in 'single quotes'.
TV shows, radio shows, movies, books and
LP titles are in *italics*.
Page numbers in **bold** refer to illustrations.

Abbey Road studio *see* EMI
"Acid Tests" 45
'Act Naturally' 58, 61
Adderley, Cannonball 12
Adventures Of Ozzie & Harriet, The 27
Airline brand 18
'Albatross' 9
Ali, Muhammad 39
'All My Loving' 51, 58
'All You Need Is Love' 32, 55
Almeida, Laurindo 27
Alray 69
AM radio 27
Ampeg 21, 23, 74, 75, 76
 ads **74, 76**
 and Burns 76
 Dan Amstrong "Black" 75, **75/76**
 Dan Armstrong "See-Through" 74, **74/75**, 75
'And Your Bird Can Sing' 56, 82
Andrew, Sam 47
'Angie' 6
Animals, The 5, **5**,
'Another Girl' 56
'Anyway, Anyhow, Anywhere' 6
Aoxomoxoa **49**
'Apache' 4, 78
Apple boutique 49
A&R man 77, 80
Arai 64, 65, 69
Arai, Shiro **64**
Archies, The 32
'Are You Experienced' 83
Are You Experienced 8, 83
Aria/Aria Diamond 64, 65, 69
 ADSG-12T **64**
 catalogue **64**
Armstrong, Dan 21, 75, 76
Armstrong, E.H. 31
Armstrong, Neil 73
Asahi Shimbun (newspaper) **66**
Astro *see* Rickenbacker
Astronauts, The 65
Atkins, Chet 5, 16, **17**, 51, 58, **60**
Atlantic 73, 82
Avalon Ballroom 45
Axis: Bold As Love 8
Axton, Estelle 73

Bacharach, Burt 44
'Badge' 30
Bain, Bob 27
Baldwin (*see also* Burns) 23, 24, 60
 ad **23**
 catalogue **23**
 Marvin **23**
 purchase Burns 23, 24
ban on guitars in Japan 66, 67
Band, The 9, 63
Barnes, George 20
Barrett, Syd 9
Barry, John Seven 6, 25
Bartolini 25
Baugh, Phil 61
Bay Of Pigs 15
BBC radio sessions 29
Beach Boys, The **26**, 45, 78-80, 81, **81**
Beatles, The **4**, 25, 28, 29, 44, 50-57, **50**, 58, 64, 65, 67-68, 69, 77, 80, 82
 (*see also* Harrison, Lennon, McCartney)
 'A Day In The Life' radio ban 49
 on BBC radio 29, 49
 distorted guitars 9
 on *Ed Sullivan Show* 28, 32, 51
 in Hamburg 51
 on *Juke Box Jury* 29
 on *Our World* 32, 55
 and Rickenbacker 5, 17, 39
 songwriting 4, 44
bebop 12, 14, 15
Beck, Jeff 7, 10, 44, **44**, 45, 47, 83
'Beck's Bolero' 44
Bell, Vinnie 61, **61**
Bennett, Wayne 72
Benson, George 14, **14**
Berlin Wall 15
Berry, Chuck 5
Berry, Dave 5

Best, Pete 51
Biba store 45
 logo **45**
Big Brother & The Holding Company 47
Bigsby 36, 53, 54
Bigsby, Paul 36
'Birthday' 57
Bishop, Elvin 82
black power 63
Blackburn, Tony 31
'Blackwater Side' 6, 10
Bland, Bobby 72
Blonde On Blonde 62
Bloomfield, Mike 47, 70, 76, 82
Blue Comets, The 67, **67**, 69
Blue Jeans, The (Japan) 65, **65**
Blue Jeans, The (US) 78, 79
blues 70-76
"blues boom" 9
Blues Breakers With Eric Clapton 7, 75, **75**
Blues Is King **73**
Bluesbreakers 6, 7, 9, 45, 75
Bogle, Bob 79, 80
Bond, James 25
Booker T & The MGs 8, 73, 80
Bradley, Harold 58, 60
Brewis, David 45
Bringing It All Back Home 6
British guitars 23, 24
"British Invasion" 28, 32
Brown, James 44, 74, 76, **76**
Bryant, Jimmy 47, **47**
"bubblegum" music 32
Buckaroos, The 60, 61
Buegeleisen & Jacobson 67
'Burning Of The Midnight Lamp' 9
Burns (*see also* Baldwin) 23, 24, 32, 69
 and Ampeg 23, 76
 Bison **22/23**
 catalogue **22**
 Jazz Split Sound **76**
 Marvin **22**
 purchased by Baldwin 23, 24
 and The Shadows 22, 23
 Split Sonic **22**
 Vista Sonic **22**
Burns, Jim 23
Burton, James 27, 44, 61, 62, 63, **63**
Butterfield Blues Band 6, 47, 82, **82**
Byrds, The 6, 17, 38, 39, 47, 58, 62, 63

Caddy, Alan 77
Caiola, Al **19**
Cameron, Dave 'Tex' 77
Campbell, Donald 49
Campbell, Glen 44
Campbell, Little Milton 72
Captain Beefheart & His Magic Band 10
'Caravan' 80
Carllile, Thumbs 26, **26**, 60
Carnaby Street 41
Carson, Bill 43
Carthy, Martin 6
Carvin 17
cassette tape 45
Catch Me 14, 15, **15**
Catch-22 15
'Certain Girl, A' 6
Chandler, Chas 76
Chantays, The 45
Chevrolet Corvette Stingray 35, **35**
Chicago Musical Instrument Co *see* CMI
"chicken-picking" 61
Churchill, Walter **28**
Clapton, Eric 30, **75**
 and The Band 9
 and The Beatles 57, 82
 and blues boom 71, 76
 blues influence 7, 45
 in Cream 7-8, 9, 82
 and The Fool 49
 and Freddy King 7, 75
 and fuzz box 6
 and George Harrison 57
 and Gibson
  ES-335 30, **30**, 35
  Firebird I 35
  Les Paul 7, 35, 57, 75, 76
  SG Standard 35, 48, 49, **49**
 and Jimmy Page 10
 and John Mayall 6-7, 45, 75
 and wah-wah 9

and "woman tone" 8, 82
 in Yardbirds 6, 45, 82
Clark, Dick 27, 31
Clark, Jim 41
Clay, Cassius 39
Cline, Patsy 58
CMI 36, 39
Cochran, Eddie 13, 53
Columbia 66
Concorde 73
Connery, Sean 25
contraceptive pill 15
Cooke, Sam 71
Coral Sitar 9, 19, 60, **60/61**, 61, **61**
Coryell, Larry 15
Country Joe & The Fish 47
country music 58-63
'Country Pie' 62
Cox, Mick 45
Crawdaddy Club 75
Cream 7-8, 9, 30, 48, 82
Creation, The 7, 49
Cropper, Steve 8, 44, 73, **73**, 80
Crosby, David 62
Crucianelli 23, 25
'Crying Game, The' 5
Cuba 15, 28
Curtis, Sonny 44
Custom Kraft 17
 ad **17**
Cutler, Stan 9
Czechoslovakia 63

Dale, Dick 44, 45, **45**
Dan Armstrong (*see also* Armstrong, Ampeg)
 Modified Danelectro **76**
Danelectro 19, 60, 61 (*see also* Coral)
 amp-in-case guitar *see* Silvertone
 Bellzouki 61
 and Dan Armstrong 76
 and MCA 60, 76
 and Sears/Silvertone 19
 sitar *see* Coral
Daniel, Nat(han) 19
Daniels, Charlie 62
D'Aquisto, Jimmy 17
David, Hal 44
Davies, Dave 5, 45
Davis, Miles 10, 12, 15
'Day In The Life, A' 49, 82
'Day Tripper' 81
DeArmond 5
Denney, Dick **59**
'Diamond Head' 65
Diddley, Bo 74
Dietrich, Ray 33, 35
"direct injection" 77
Disraeli Gears 48, 82, **82**
'Distant Drums' 59
distortion 6, 78 (*see also* fuzz)
Dobro 18
Domino 58, 65
 ad **58**
 California Rebel **58/59**
'Don't Worry' 58
Dowd, Tom 82
Dr No 25
Dreja, Chris 83
Dudgeon, Gus 7
Du Pont 42
Dylan, Bob 6, 15, 47, 62, 63, **63**

Eagles, The (UK) **22**
Eagles, The (US) 63
'East-West' 82
East-West 82
Ecco-Fonic 58
Echoplex 58
ECL 39
Ed Sullivan Show, The 28, 32, 50, 51, 53
Eddy, Duane 27, **27**, 61, 81
Edge (U2) 15
Edmunds, Dave 9, 29
Edwards, Nokie 36, 61, 80
Egmond 24
'Eight Miles High' 17, 38
Eko 23, 24, 25, 40
 catalogue **25**
El Hombre **15**
Electric Lady studios 83
Electric Ladyland 8, 43

Eleki No Wakadaisho 65
Elk 66
 Deluxe 66
Elpico 5
Emergency 83, **83**
Emerick, Geoff 80
EMI studios (Abbey Road) 57, 77, 78, 80, **80**, 82
'End, The' 57
Engelhardt, Robert **28**
Epiphone 31, 39
 ads **18**, **19**
 Casino **52/53/54**, 53, **53**, **53/54**, 56
 catalogue **19**
 Sheraton **18/19**
Erickson, Roky 49
European guitars 22-25
Evans, David (Edge) 15
Evans, Mal 56
Everett, Kenny 31
Evolution 46
Excetro 69
Extrapolation **15**

Fairport Convention 9
feedback 6, 7, 56
Fender 22, 40-43, 73
 ads **26**, **40**, **42**, **43**, **46**, **73**
 Antigua finish 46
 "Arrow" 43
 Bassman amp 70
 Bronco 43
 catalogues **32**, **40**, **41**
 Coronado line 42, 46
  XII Wildwood II **46**
 Custom 43, 73
 custom colors 42
 delivery truck **41**
 Electric XII 41, **41**, 43
 Esquire 57
 Jaguar 26, **26/27**, 41, **41**
 Jazzmaster 23, **43**, 59
 LTD 43
 Marauder 40, **40/41**, 41, **41**
 Maverick 43
 Montego 43
 Musiclander 43
 Mustang 41
 purchase by CBS 32, 41-42, 42
 Stratocaster 4, 6, 8, 22, 24, 42, **42**, **42/43**, 43, **43**, 45, 55, **55/56/57**, 56, 57, 70, 71, 78
 Swinger 43
 Telecaster 8, 43, 58, 61, 62, 63, 73
  Blue Flower 43, 63, **63**
  Paisley Red 43, **62/63**, 63
  Rosewood 43, **57**, 72, **72/73**
  Thinline 43
 Wildwood finish 42, 46
Fender, Leo 40, 41, **41**, 42
fibreglass 18, 28
Fillmore Auditorium 45
Finch, Barry 49
Fingers, The **69**
Firstman 67, 69
 catalogue **67**
 Liverpool-67 model 67, **67**, 69
'Fixing A Hole' 57
Fleerekkers, The 77
Fleetwood Mac 9
Flick, Vic 6, 25
Flying Burrito Brothers, The 63
FM radio 31-32
folk/folk-rock 6, 27, 40-41, 42, 47
Fool, The 48, 49
Fool, The (LP) **49**
For Django 14
'For Your Love' 82
Ford, Mary **21**
Fordyce, Keith 29
Formby, George 15
Framus 23, 25, 68
 ad **25**
 Attila Zoller 25
 Strato Deluxe **25**
Free 9
Freed, Alan 27
Fresh Cream 8
Fripp, Robert 10
Frost, Al 18
Fujigen Gakki 65
Full House 12
'Fun, Fun, Fun' 81

funk guitar 74
fusion *see* jazz-rock
Fusion 12
Futurama 23, 37, **51** (*see also* Neoton)
fuzz box/pedal 6, 7, 44, 58, 78
Fuzz Face 83

Gagarin, Yuri 15
Galanti 23, 61
　Grand Prix **61**
'Games People Play' 61
Garcia, Jerry 47, 48, **49**
Garland, Hank 58, **58**, 59, 60-61
Gemelli 25
　catalogue **25**
Germany 23
'Getting Better' 57
Gibson 33-39
　ads **21**, **33**, **71**
　Barney Kessel **14/15**, 34
　Byrdland 39
　catalogues **20**, **31**, **35**
　Citation 39
　custom color chart **33**
　double-neck 34
　EBSF-1250 6
　ES-335 **30/31**, 33, 39, 59, 70
　ES-345 56, 59
　ES-355 **31**, 59
　factory 35, **35**
　Firebird 33-36
　　"non-reverse" body 34, 35, 36
　　"reverse" body 34, 36
　　I **34/35**, **35**
　　III 35
　　V **33/34/35**, 35, **35**
　　VII **34**, 35, **35**
　Flying V 39, 44, **44/45**, 45
　Fuzztone *see* Maestro
　J-160E **52**, 53, 54, **54**
　Johnny Smith 15, 34
　L-5CES 11, **11/12**, 39
　Les Paul 6, 9, 24, 44, **56/57**, 57, 71
　　Custom 9, 39, 71, **71**
　　Deluxe 39
　　gold-top 6, 9, 39, 57, 70, 71, 75
　　Jumbo 39
　　Personal 39, 72, **72/73**
　　Professional 39, 72
　　reissues 9, 39, 71
　　Sunburst (aka Standard) 6, 9, 34, 39, 71, 75, 76
　Melody Maker 34, 39
　and Norlin 39
　purchase of CMI by ECL 39
　SG line 34, 35
　　Junior 39
　　Special **21**
　　Standard 39, **48/49**, 55, 56
　SG/Les Paul
　　Custom **20/21**
　　Standard **20/21**, 34
　sharp "Florentine" cutaway 11, 34
　Super 400CES 11, 14, 39
　Tal Farlow **15**, 34
　Trini Lopez 34, 39, **39**
Gibson, Don 58
Goin' Out Of My Head 13
Gold Star studio 78
'Gone With The Wind' 77
'Good Morning Good Morning' 57
'Good Vibrations' 79
Goodbye Cream 30
Goya 37, 40, 65
　logo **40**
　Rangemaster **40/41**
Grateful Dead, The 45, 47, 48, 49
"Great" Train Robbery 35
Greco 40, 69
Green, Peter 9, **9**, 71
'Green Onions' 8, 73, 80
Green Onions **80**
'Green Tambourine' 9, 61
Green Tambourine **61**
Gretsch 17-18
　Astro-Jet **32**
　Bikini 17
　catalogue **32**
　Chet Atkins Country Gentleman 16, **16/17**, 50, **50**, 51, **52**, 60
　Chet Atkins Hollow Body 20
　Corvette **32**

custom model 55
double-cutaway body 16, 17, 32
Duo Jet **51**, 52
factory 17, **17**
Monkees 44, **44**
Nashville 55, 57
Princess **32**
Tennessean 53
Twist 32
White Falcon 18, **31/32**
12-string 17
6120 *see* Chet Atkins Hollow Body
Gretty, Jim 54
"Group Sounds" 65, 68, 69
GS *see* Group Sounds
Guild 27
　AcoustiLectric 20
　Bert Weedon Model **37**
　Bluesbird 20
　Duane Eddy 20, **27**
　Guitar In F 21
　Starfire 20
　Stratford 20
　Thunderbird S200 **37**
Gurley, James 47
Guy, Buddy 70, 71, **71**
Guyatone 41, 65, 69
　and Kent 67
　LG-65T 65
　LG-200T 41, **41**, 65-66
　LG-350T Sharp Five 69
　SG-42T 69

Haggard, Merle 61-62, **61**, 62, 63
Hagström 23, 40
　catalogue **37**
　and Elvis Presley 37
　Kent PB24G **37**
　Viking **37**
Hagström, Albin 37
Hall, F.C. (Francis) 38, **38**, 53
'Happiness Is A Warm Gun' 57
'Hard Day's Night, A' 5, 17, 51, 56
Harmony 13, 20, 69
　catalogues **13**, **19**
　Meteor 5, **12/13**, 13
　Rocket **19**, 21
Harries, Dave 82
Harrison, George **50**, **51**, **52**, 80, **80**, 82
　and Epiphone 53, 56
　and Eric Clapton 57
　and Fender 55, 56, 57, **57**, 72
　and Gibson 52, 53, 54, **54**, 55, 56, 57
　and Gretsch 16, **50**, 51, 52, **52**, 53, 55, **55**, 57, 58
　and Neoton/Futurama 51, **51**, 52
　and Rickenbacker 5, 17, 39, 50, 51, 53, 55, 56
　and sitar 7, 60
　and Vox 55
'Heart Full Of Soul' 7, 44
Heinz **77**
Heit 65
'He'll Have To Go' 58
Helland, Dan 59
Heller, Joseph 15
Hendrickson, Al 27
Hendrix, Jimi **8**, **43**, **44**, 47-48, 76, **76**, 83, **83**
　detuned guitar 8
　backwards recording 8
　and Flying V 39, 44, **44**, 45
　as rhythm guitarist 8, 76
　signs to Warner-Reprise 49
　and Stratocaster 8, 24, 43, **43**
　vibrato system use 8
　and wah-wah pedal 9, 78
'Here, There And Everywhere' 56
Herr, Michael 73
Herston, Kelso 59, 60
Hessy's music shop 54
Hicks, Tony 46, **46**, 78, **78**
hi-fi 27
Hillman, Chris 62, 63
Hinton, Eddie 74
"hippie" bands 47
Hitchcock, Alfred 13
Höfner 11, 22, 23, 50, **51**, 67
　Club models 23, 52
　Galaxie 23
　Verithin 11, **11**, 23
Hollies, The 46, 78, **78**
Holman 59, 69

Holman-Woodell 59
Honey 69
　SG-5 69
Hootenanny 27, 31
Hopf 23
Hoshino Gakki 65
Hot Rats 10, **10**
'House Of The Rising Sun, The' 5, 28
Howe, Steve 9
Howlin' Wolf 70, 71, 77
Huis, John 36
Hull, Everett 75
Huston, Chris 54
Hunters, The **24**
Hurst, Gary 6

'I Am The Walrus' 55
'I Can't Explain' 6, 17, 39
'I Feel Fine' 56
'I Feel Free' 8
'I Found A Love' 72
'I Love You Because' 59
'I Should Have Known Better' 56
'I Wanna Be Your Man' 4
Ibanez 65
Idol 69
'I'm A Lonesome Fugitive' 62
I'm A Lonesome Fugitive **61**
'I'm Moving On' 63
'I'm Only Sleeping' 56
In A Silent Way 15
In The Court Of The Crimson King 10, **10**
Incredible Jazz Guitar Of Wes Montgomery, The **11**, 12
Indian music 7, 9, 14, 15, 60
Ingmann, Jørgen **78**
International Times 45
Israel 49
Italian guitars 23, 25, 61
'Itchycoo Park' 60
It's Uptown **14**
'I've Just Seen A Face' 63
Iwase, Yukichi 66

Jackson, Leo 59, **59**
Jaguar (brand) 69
Jamerson, James 72
James, Etta 73
Jammed Together **73**
Jansch, Bert 6, 10
Japanese guitars 24, 25, 38, 41, 58, 64-69
jazz 11-15
jazz-rock 10, 14, 15, 83
Jazz Winds From A New Direction 58
Jeff Beck Group, The 44
Jefferson Airplane 47, 48
John Wesley Harding 62, 63
Johnson, Jimmy 74
Johnson, Lyndon B. 39, 41
Jones, Brian 7, **22**, 31, **34**, 44, 73
Jones, George 60
Jones, Ralph 70
Jones, Spike 41
Juke Box Jury 29
'Just One look' 78

Kachinuki Eleki Gassen 66
Kalamazoo ad **35**
Kasuga Gakki 65
Katz, Sidney 21
Kaukonen, Jorma 47, 48
Kawai 38, 58, 65, 67
　"amp-in-guitar" 38, **38/39**
　Concert **67**
　and Kent 67
　and Telestar 68
　purchase Teisco 65, 67, 69
Kay 17, 20, 21
　ads **17**, **67**
　catalogue **21**
　factory **21**
　Jazz II 20
　and Seeburg purchase 21
　and Valco 18, 21, 29
Kay, John 83
Kayama, Yuzo 65, **65**
Keeler, Christine 35
'Keep On Running' 7
Keepnews, Orrin 12
Kennedy, Jerry 59, 81
Kennedy, John F. 15, 28, 35

Kennedy, Robert 63
Kent 45, 65, 67
　ad **45**
　742 model 66, **66/67**
Kessel, Barney **15**
Kidd, Johnny & The Pirates 4
Kim Sisters, The **29**
King, Albert 70, 73
King, B.B. 70, 73, **73**
King, Freddy 7, 70, 71, 74, **74**, 75, 77
King, Martin Luther 35, 63
King Crimson 10
Kingston 65
Kinks, The 5, **6**, **28**, 45
Kirshner, Don 32
Kirwan, Danny 9
Klira 23
KMPX 31
Knock Me Out! **80**
Koger, Marijke 49
Kooper, Al 43
Kossoff, Paul 9
Kramer, Eddie 83
Kustom 69
　K200C **69**

La Baye 59
　2-By-4 **59**
Lady Chatterley's Lover 13
'Last Train To Clarksville, The' 44
Lawrence, Bill 21
Lawrence, D.H. 13
Lawrence Welk Show, The 27
Leary, Dr Timothy 35
Led Zeppelin 9-10, 45
Led Zeppelin II 9
Lee, Alvin 9
Leeger, Josje 49
Lemon Pipers, The 9, 61
Lennon, John **50**, **52**, **53**, 80, **80**, 82
　and Bigsby 54
　and Epiphone 53, **53**, 56, 57
　and Fender 56, 57
　and The Fool 49
　and Gibson 52, **52**, 53, 54, **54**, 57
　and Gretsch 55, 57
　and Höfner 52
　and Rickenbacker **50**, 51, 53, 54, 55
Leonov, Alexei 41
Les Paul guitar *see* Gibson
Les Paul Now! 21
Leslie cabinet 9, 57, 82
'Let It Be' 57
'Let's Go Trippin' 45
Let's Hide Away And Dance Away 7, **74**, 75
Levin 69
Levine, Larry 78
Liberty 69
'Licking Stick' 76
Lifetime 15, 83
Lindley, David 69
Lipsky 23, 58
'Little Sister' 58, 61
Lo Duca 25
London 45
Lopez, Trini 34, 39, **39**
Lotus 49
Love Sculpture 9, 29
Lovin' Spoonful, The 62
LSD 7, 35, 45, 47
'Lucy In The Sky With Diamonds' 9, 57
'Lullaby Of The Leaves' 79

Maccaferri, Mario 52, **52**
Maestro Fuzztone 6, **6**, 58
Maghett *see* Magic Sam
'Magic Carpet Ride' 83
Magic Sam 70, 71, **71**
Magnatone catalogue **19**
Mahavishnu Orchestra 15
Mailer, Norman 35
Man & The Blues, A **71**
Man From UNCLE, The 39, **39**
Manfred Mann 28
Manley, Colin 81
Manny's music store 9
Maphis, Joe 20, 37
Marquee Club 8
Marshall amplifiers 7, 8, 8-9, 76, 78
Martin 17
　ad **17**
Martin, George 80

Martin, Grady 58, 59
Martino, Pat 14, 15, **15**
Marvin, Hank B. 4, **4**, 22, **22**, 78
Mastro 52
　ad **52**
Maton 24
　logo **24**
Matsuda, Doryu 69
Matsuki, Mitsuo 69
Mayall, John 6, 7, 9, 45, **75**
Mayfield, Curtis 72
MCA 60, 76
McCartney, Paul **50**, **52**, 80, **80**, 82
　and Epiphone 53, **53**, 56
　and Fender 57
　and Höfner 50, 53
　and Rickenbacker 56, 57
　and Rosetti 52
McCarty, Ted **19**, 36
McGee, Jerry 44
McGowan, Cathy 29
McGuinn, Roger (aka Jim) 6, **6**, 17, 39, 47, 62
McLaughlin, John 10, 15, 83
McLuhan, Marshall 26
Meek, Joe 77, **77**
Mellowtone 65
Melton, Barry 47
Memphis scale 73
Merrill, Buddy 27
Merseybeat 4
Mersey Beat magazine 54
Merson 37
Messenger 59
　ME-11 **59**
Messina, Joe 8
MGs, The 8, 73, 74
Micro-Frets 17, 70
　Calibrato 70
　Micro-Nut 70
　The Orbiter 70, **70/71**
Mihara, Tunaki 67, **67**, 69
Miller, Jerry 48
Miller, Mitch 27
Mine, Nobuhiro 69, **69**
Minister 69
Mitchell, Bill 35
Moby Grape 48
　logo **48**
Mods & Rockers 39
Monarch, Michael 83
Monkees, The 31, 32, **32**, **44**
Monterey Pop festival 47, 49
Montgomery, Wes 11, **11**, 12-14, **13**, 77, **77**, 80
Mooney, Ralph 63
Moore, Gary (US comedian) 27
Morales 65
More Real Folk Blues **72**
Moretti, Joe 4
Mory 66
Moseley, Semie 20, 37, **37**
Mosrite 20, 36, 37, 60, 65, 69
　ad **36**
　Ventures 36, **36/37**, 65, **65**, 69
Moss, Wayne 62, 81
'Mother Popcorn' 76
Motown 8, 44, 72, 73
Mourning In The Morning **70**
Movin' Wes **80**
'Mr Tambourine Man' 6, 17
Munsters, The 39, **39**
Muscle Beach Party 45
Muscle Shoals studio 74
Music From Big Pink 63
Music Supply Corp ad **65**
Musima 24
'My Generation' 6

'Nashville Cats' 62
Nashville Skyline 62, 63, **63**
"Nashville Sound" 58, 59, 60
National 18, 29
　ad **29**
　catalogue **29**
　"map-shape" guitar 29
　Newport-84 **28/29**
　plastic guitars 18, 28
　Res-O-Glas 18, 27
"needle time" 29
Nelson, Ricky 27, 63, **63**
Neoton Grazioso 51, **51**, 52
Neville, Richard 49
Nichol, Al **61**

Nichols, Roy 61-62
Nolen, Jimmy 44, 74, 76, **76**
Northern Ireland 73
'Norwegian Wood' 60
'Nowhere Man' 56

Oahu 18
Olympic studios 83
op-art 16, 41
O'Rahilly, Ronan 29
Orbison, Roy 59, 81
Oswald, Lee Harvey 35
Out Cast, The 65
Ovation 17
　ad **17**
Owens, Buck 58, 60, **60**, 61, 62, 63
　and Fender Telecaster 58, 61
Oz 49, **49**

Page, Jimmy 6, 7, **9**, 9-10, 45, 60
'Paint It Black' 7
'Papa's Got A Brand New Bag' 74, 76
'Paperback Writer' 53, 80
Parsons, Gram 62
Parsons-White B-Bender 63
Pass, Joe 14, 15, **15**
Paul, Les 21, **21**, 34, 72, 78
payola 27
Peel, John 29, 31
Perine, Bob 40
Pet Sounds 80, 81
'Peter Gunn' 81
"phasing" 60
Phillips, Eddie 7, **7**, 10
Pickett, Wilson 72
Pink Floyd 8, 9, 49
'Pipeline' 45
pirate radio 31
plastic 18, 21, 25, 28, 37, 74, 75
Play In A Day 37
Playboys, The 65
Pleasant 66
Poco 63
pop music 44-49
Porter, Dean 59
Posthuma, Simon 49
Powers, Gary 13, 28
Presley, Elvis 13, **37**, 58, 61, 62, 63, 73
'Pretty Woman, Oh' 59, 81
Profumo, John 35
"progressive" rock 10
psychedelia 7
Psychedelic Shop 45
Psychedelic Sounds Of 13th Floor Elevators 49
Psycho 13

Quant, Mary 45
Quick One, A **39**
Quonset Hut studio 58, 60

'Race Is On, The' 60
radio 26-32
Radio Caroline 31, **31**
Radio Luxembourg 29, 77
Rajah Zeetar 60
　ad **60**
Randall, Don 40, 42, 43
R&B 4, 6
Reading, Doyle 69
Ready, Steady, Go! 28, **28**, 28-29
recording 77-83
Reed, Jimmy 70
Reeves, Jim 58, 59, **59**
Regal 41
Remo Four, The 81
Renbourn, John 6
Rendell, Stanley 36, 39
Res-O-Glas *see* National
Revere, Paul & The Raiders 31
'Revolution' 57
Revolver 45, 56, 82, **82**
Rich, Don 60, **60**, 61
Richards, Keith 5, **12**, 44, 78
Rickenbacker 16, 50, 51, 53, 59, 69
　ad **38**
　Astro AS-51 **38**
　catalogues **16**, **38**
　Convertible 17
　and Rose-Morris (UK) 25, 38
　stereo guitar 17
　12-string 5, 6, 17, 38-39, 50-51, 53
　325 model 50, **50**, **50/51**, 53

325/12 model 55
360/12 model **50/51**
360S/12 "1993" model **38/39**
425 model 55
460 model **16**
Riley, Bridget 16
Robbins, Marty 58
Roberts, Dave 59
Robertson, Robbie 9
Robinson, Smokey 72
rock music 44-49
Rolling Stones, The 4, 7, 9, 44, 63, 78
Rose-Morris 25, 38
　catalogue **38**
Rosetti 53
　Solid-7 52
Rossmeisl, Roger 41, 42
Rubovits, Chuck 20
Ruby, Jack 35
Rundgren, Todd 48
Rush, Otis 70, **70**
Rushworth's music shop 54

'Sabre Dance' 9, 29
San Francisco 45, 47
Sanford, Billy 81
Santana, Carlos 10
'Satisfaction, (I Can't Get No)' 7, 78, 81
'Satisfied Mind' 62
Screen Gems 44
'Sea Of Heartbreak' 58
Sears 19, 20, 29
Seeburg 21
Selmer 20
　catalogue **20**
'Sexy Sadie' 57
Sgt Pepper's Lonely Hearts Club Band 56-57, 80, 82
Shadows, The 4, **4**, 22, **22**, **32**, 44, 77, 78, **78**
Shaftesbury 25
'Shakin All Over' 4
'Shapes Of Things' 7, 83
Sharp 5, The 69, **69**
Shepherd, Alan 15
Shindig 31
shops, music 7, 9, 54
Shrimpton, Jean 41
Silvertone 18, 19
　1457 guitar/amp/case set 29, **29**
sitar 7, 9, 19, 60, 61
"sit-com" 27
"slack-stringing" 7
Slash (Guns N'Roses) 41
'Slaughter On Tenth Avenue' 80
Small Faces, The 60
Smile 80
Smokin' At The Half Note 80
Smothers Brothers 32
Snoddy, Glenn 58
Snow, Hank 63
So Much Guitar! **11**
'Something' 57
soul music 70-76
Sound Of Music, The 41
South, Joe 61, 62
South Africa 13, 25
Soxx, Bob B & The Blue Jeans 78, 79
Spector, Phil 44, 78, **79**
'Spectrum' 83
Spencer, Jeremy 9
Spencer Davis Group, The 7, 77
Spiderman 25, **25**
Spiders, The 65
Splender 66
'Spoonful' 77
Spotnicks, The 10, **24**, **32**
Springfield, Tom 50
St Louis Music 17
"stack" amplifier 8-9
'Stand By Your Man' 59
Staple Singers, The 74
Staples, Pops 73, 74
Star 65
Stax 8, 44, 73, 82
Stephens, John 45
Steppenwolf 83
Steppenwolf Second **83**
stereo radio 31
stereo system 27
Stewart, Jim 73
'Stone Free' 8
stores *see* shops

Strange, Billy 79
Strangers, The 61
Stratocaster *see* Fender
string-bending 7, 15
string gauges 8
studio *see* recording
Sullivan, Ed 28, 29, **29**
Sumlin, Hubert 71, 77
'Sunday Date' 77
'Sunshine Of Your Love' 82
Supro 18
surf music 45, 65
Surfaris, The 45
'Surfin USA' 45
Sutcliffe, Stuart **51**
Suzuki 66
Sweetheart Of The Rodeo 62, **62**, 63
Swing West 65

'Tales Of Brave Ulysses' 9
Tamla, Tamla Motown *see* Motown
Tarplin, Marv 8, 72
'Taxman' 56
Taylor, Mick 9
Tedesco, Tommy 27, **27**, 31
Teisco/Teisco Del Rey 47, 65
　catalogue **47**
　Fire Bird 69
　and Firstman 67, 69
　and Honey 69
　K series 68
　logo **65**, **69**
　May Queen **64/65**, 69
　Phantom 69
　purchase by Kawai 65, 67, 69
　SM series 68
　Spectrum-5 **47**, 68
　TG-64 65
　TRG-1 38, 65
　V series 68
　Vamper 69
　and WMI 47
Telestar catalogue **68**
television *see* TV
Telstar (satellite) 25
'Telstar' (record) 77
Ten Years After 9
Terauchi, Takeshi 65
"test-tube baby" 73
Thomas Organ 9
Thompson, Richard 9
Thunderbirds **32**
'Ticket To Ride' 53, 56, 80
'Tiger By The Tail' 61
Titov, Gherman 15
Tokai 69
　Humming Bird **68/69**
Tokyo Sound Co 69
Tombo 66
Tomorrow 9, 49
'Tomorrow Never Knows' 80
Tone Bender 6, 7
Top Gear 29
Top Of The Pops 29
Topham, Top 75
Tornados, The 77
Townshend, Pete 6, **6**, 39, **39**, 45
'Tracks Of My Tears, The' 72
transistor radio 27
tremolo arm *see* vibrato system 8
Trout Mask Replica 10
TTG studio 83, **83**
Turtles, The 61
TV 26-32
Twiggy 41
twist (dance) 15

Undead 9
"underground" radio 31-32
"underground" rock 9, 31
Undertakers, The 54
U2 spy plane 13, 28

Valco 18, 21, 28, 29 (*see also* National)
　factory **28**
Ventures, The 36, **36**, 44, 61, 65, 66-67, 69, 78, 79, **79**, 80
Vernon, Mike 7, 75
Vietnam 15, 28, 39, 41, 63, 73
vibrato 7
vibrato system 8, 79
Victor 66

Voice 66
    Frontier Custom-1000 66
Vox 22, 23, 24-25
    amplifiers 4, 50, 78
    custom model 55
    and Eko 24
    factory (England) **46**
    Guitar Organ 46, **46/47**
    Italian production 24, 46
    Mando Guitar 65
    Marauder **59**
    Mark 22, **22**, 23, 31
    Phantom 23
        XII **46**
    "teardrop" guitar *see* MkVI
    and Thomas Organ 46
    US operation 46
    Voxmobile 47, **47**
    wah-wah pedal **8**, 9, 83
    Winchester 59, **59**
wah-wah pedal **8**, 9
'Walk – Don't Run' 36, 65, 78
"Wall Of Sound" 78

Wallace, George 35
Wandré 23
    Rock Oval **24/25**
Ward, Robert 72
Waters, Muddy 70, 71, 72, **72**
Watkins (*see also* WEM, Wilson) 23, 24
    amplifiers 23
    catalogue **23**
    Circuit-4 **23**
    Rapier-33 **23**
Watkins, Charlie 23
Weedon, Bert **12**, 22, 37
Weir, Bob 45, 47, 48
Welch, Bruce 77, 78
WEM 23, 24
    logo **23**
Wes Montgomery Trio, The 12
'West Coast Blues' 80
West Side blues 70, 71
West Side Soul **71**
Wexler, Jerry 73
"whammy" bar *see* vibrato system
'What Goes On' 63

Wheels Of Fire **48**
Where The Action Is 31
'While My Guitar Gently Weeps' 57, 82
White, Clarence 62, **62**, 63
White, Robert 8
Who, The 6, 10, 17, 39, 45, 47
'Whole Lotta Love' 32
Williams, Tony 10, 15, 83
Willis, Eddie 8
Wilson 23, 24
Wilson, Brian 78-80, **81**
Wilson, Carl 26, **26**, 81
Wilson, Don 79, 80
Winston 65
Winwood, Muff 77
'Wipe Out' 45
Womack, Bobby 72
"woman tone" 8, 82
Woodstock Music & Art Fair 10, 73
Woolf, Maurice 38, **38**
Wurlitzer 18, 59
    ad **18**
Wynette, Tammy 59

Yamada, Yukiho 66
Yamaha 68, 69
    catalogue 68
Yardbirds, The 6, 7, 9, 44, 45, 47, 75, 83
'You Can't Do That' 5, 17, 53
'You Really Got A Hold On Me' 72
'You Really Got Me' 5, 28
Young, Chip 60

Zappa, Frank 10
Zen-on Gakki 65
Zenon 65, 66
'Zip-A-Dee-Do-Dah' 78, 79

12-string guitar 5, 38, 61, 64
13th Floor Elevators 49
14-Hour Technicolor Dream 49
21st Century (brand) 59
'21st Century Schizoid Man' 10
2001: A Space Odyssey 63

BIBLIOGRAPHY

Tony Bacon (ed) *Classic Guitars Of The Fifties* (Balafon/Miller Freeman 1996)
Tony Bacon & Paul Day *The Fender Book* (Balafon/Miller Freeman 1992), *The Gibson Les Paul Book* (Balafon/Miller Freeman 1993), *The Gretsch Book* (Balafon/Miller Freeman 1996), *The Rickenbacker Book* (Balafon/Miller Freeman 1994), *The Ultimate Guitar Book* (DK/Knopf 1991)
Tony Bacon & Barry Moorhouse *The Bass Book* (Balafon/Miller Freeman 1995)
Paul Bechtholdt & Doug Tulloch *Guitars From Neptune – A Definitive Journey into Danelectro Mania* (Backporch 1995)
Julius Bellson *The Gibson Story* (Gibson 1973)
Harry Benson *The Beatles In The Beginning* (Mainstream 1993)
British Film Institute *British Television* (Oxford University Press 1994)
Tim Brooks & Earle Marsh *The Complete Directory To Prime Time Network TV Shows 1946-Present* (Ballantine 1979)
Bill Bryson *Made In America* (Secker & Warburg 1994)
Walter Carter *Epiphone: The Complete History* (Hal Leonard 1995)
Scott Chinery & Tony Bacon *The Chinery Collection – 150 Years Of American Guitars* (Balafon/Miller Freeman 1996)
Alan Clayson *Beat Merchants – Origins, History, Impact, Rock Legacy of 1960s British Pop Groups* (Blandford 1995)
Richard Cook & Brian Morton *The Penguin Guide To Jazz on CD, LP and Cassette* (Penguin 1994)
Country Music Magazine *The Complete US Country Music Encyclopedia* (Boxtree 1995)
Mark Cunningham *Good Vibrations – A History Of Record Production* (Castle 1996)
Paul Day *The Burns Book* (PP 1979)
Robert & Celia Dearling *Guinness Book Of Recorded Sound* (Guinness 1984)
Chris Dreja et al *Yardbirds* (Sidgwick & Jackson 1983)
A.R. Duchossoir *The Fender Stratocaster* (Mediapresse 1988), *The Fender Telecaster* (Hal Leonard 1991), *Gibson Electrics - The Classic Years* (Hal Leonard 1994)
Andrew J. Edelstein *The Swinging Sixties* (World Almanac 1985)
Jeff Evans *The Guinness Television Encyclopedia* (Guinness 1995)
Mo Foster *Seventeen Watts – The First 20 Years of British Rock Guitar* (Sanctuary 1997)
Pete Frame *The Beatles and Some Other Guys – Rock Family Trees of the Early Sixties* (Omnibus 1997), *The Complete Rock Family Trees* (Omnibus 1993)
George Fullerton *Guitar Legends: The Evolution Of The Guitar From Fender To G&L* (Centerstream 1993)
Paul Gambaccini et al *The Guinness Book Of British Hit Singles* (Guinness 1979)
Ken Garner *In Session Tonight – The Complete Radio 1 Recordings* (BBC 1993)
Charlie Gillett *The Sound Of The City* (Souvenir 1996)
Gordon Giltrap & Neville Marten *The Hofner Guitar* (IMP 1993)
Robert Gordon *It Came From Memphis* (Secker & Warburg 1995)
Hugh Gregory *1000 Great Guitarists* (Balafon/Miller Freeman 1994)

George Gruhn & Walter Carter *Electric Guitars And Basses* (GPI 1994), *Gruhn's Guide To Vintage Guitars* (GPI 1991)
Guitar Magazine 'Mooks' *Bizarre Guitars* (Rittor 1993)
Peter Guralnick *Sweet Soul Music* (Harper 1986)
Phil Hardy & Dave Laing *The Faber Companion To 20th-Century Popular Music* (Faber 1990)
Bill Harry (ed) *Mersey Beat: The Beginnings Of The Beatles* (Omnibus 1977)
Fred Heggeness *Goldmine Country Western Record & CD Price Guide* (Krause 1996)
David Heslam (ed) *NME Rock'n'Roll Decades: The Sixties* (W.H. Smith/Octopus 1992)
David Holloway (ed) *The Daily Telegraph: The Sixties* (Simon & Schuster 1992)
Terry Hounsome *Rock Record 7* (RRP 1997)
Barney Hoskyns *Waiting for the Sun – The Story of the Los Angeles Music Scene* (Viking 1996)
Steve Howe & Tony Bacon *The Steve Howe Guitar Collection* (Balafon/Miller Freeman 1994)
Kevin Howlett *The Beatles At The BBC – The Radio Years 1962-1970* (BBC 1996)
Information Please *Almanac, Atlas & Yearbook 1997* (Houghton & Mifflin 1997)
Adrian Ingram *Wes Montgomery* (Ashley Mark 1985)
JTG *Gibson Shipping Totals 1946-1979* (JTG 1992)
Barry Kernfeld (ed) *The New Grove Dictionary Of Jazz* (Macmillan 1994)
Rich Kienzle *Great Guitarists* (Facts on File 1985)
Colin Larkin (ed) *The Guinness Encyclopedia Of Popular Music* (Guinness 1992)
Spencer Leigh & John Firminger *Halfway To Paradise – Britpop 1955-1962* (Finbarr 1996)
Jon E Lewis & Penny Stempel *Cult TV* (Pavilion 1993)
Mark Lewisohn *The Complete Beatles Recording Sessions* (Hamlyn 1988), *The Complete Beatles Chronicle* (Pyramid 1992)
Dave McAleer *Beat Boom! Pop Goes The Sixties* (Hamlyn 1994), *The Book Of Hit Singles* (Carlton 1994), *Hit Parade Heroes: British Beat Before The Beatles* (Hamlyn 1993)
Alex McNeil *Total Television – The Comprehensive Guide To Programming From 1948 To The Present* (Penguin 1996)
George Melly *Owning Up* (Weidenfeld & Nicholson 1965)
Ray Minhinnett & Bob Young *The Story Of The Fender Stratocaster* (IMP 1995)
Norman Mongan *The History Of The Guitar In Jazz* (Oak 1983)
John Morrish *The Fender Amp Book* (Balafon/Miller Freeman 1995)
Hans Moust *The Guild Guitar Book 1952-1977* (GuitArchives 1995)
Michael Naglav *Höfner Guitars – Made In Germany* (Musikkeller undated c1996)
Norm N. Nite *Rock On Almanac: The First Four Decades Of Rock'n'Roll* (Harper & Row 1989)
Greg Paul *Pop Graphics 60s Style* (PBC 1995)
Gareth L. Pawlowski *How They Became The Beatles* (Dutton 1989)

David Petersen & Dick Denney *The Vox Story* (Bold Strummer 1993)
Klaus Plaumann *The Beat Age* (Zweitausendeins 1978)
Terry Rawlings & Keith Badman *Good Times Bad Times: The Definitive Diary of the Rolling Stones 1960-1969* (Complete Music 1997)
Marc Roberty *Eric Clapton – The Complete Recording Sessions 1963-1995* (St Martin's Press 1993)
Rock & Roll Hall Of Fame *I Want To Take You Higher: The Psychedelic Era 1965-1969* (Chronicle 1997)
Johnny Rogan *The Byrds: Timeless Flight* (Square One 1990)
James Sallis *The Guitar Players: One Instrument & Its Masters In American Music* (University of Nebraska Press 1982)
Darcy Sarto *Lady Don't Fall Backwards* (Eastcheam 1960)
Norbert Schnepel & Helmuth Lemme *Elektro-Gitarren Made In Germany* English translation J P Klink (Musik-Verlag Schnepel-Lemme 1988)
Harry Shapiro & Caesar Glebbeek *Jimi Hendrix: Electric Gypsy* (Heinemann 1990)
Mary Alice Shaughnessy *Les Paul: An American Original* (Morrow 1993)
David Shipman *Cinema: The First Hundred Years* (Weidenfeld & Nicholson 1995)
Richard R. Smith *Fender: The Sound Heard 'Round The World* (Garfish 1995)
Brian Southall *Abbey Road* (EMI 1982)
Maurice J. Summerfield *The Jazz Guitar: Its Evolution, Players & Personalities Since 1900* (Ashley Mark 1993)
John Tobler *This Day In Rock* (Carlton 1993)
Paul Trynka (ed) *Rock Hardware – 40 Years Of Rock Instrumentation* (Balafon/Miller Freeman 1996)
Paul Trynka & Val Wilmer *Portait Of The Blues* (Hamlyn 1996)
John Walker (ed) *Halliwell's Filmgoer's Companion* (HarperCollins 1993)
Jerry Wexler & David Ritz *Rhythm And The Blues*
Tom Wheeler *American Guitars* (HarperPerennial 1990)
Joel Whitburn *The Billboard Book of Top 40 Hits* (Billboard 1987), *Billboard's Top 10 Charts – A Week By Week History Of The Hottest Of The Hot 100 1958-1988* (Record Research 1988), *Top Pop Singles 1955-1993* (Record Research 1994), *Top 40 Country Hits* (Billboard 1996)
Forrest White *Fender, The Inside Story* (Miller Freeman 1994)
Michael Wright *Guitar Stories Volume 1: The Histories Of Cool Guitars* (Vintage Guitar Books 1995)
YMM Player *History Of Electric Guitars* (Player Corporation 1988).

MAGAZINES & PERIODICALS

We found the following useful during research: *Asahi Shimbun* newspaper; *Beat Instrumental*; *Beat Monthly*; *The Beatles Book*; *Beatles Unlimited*; *Billboard*; *Down Beat*; *Guitar Player*; *Guitar World*; *Melody Maker*; *Metronome*; *Music Trade* (Japan); *The Music Trades* (US); *Record Collector*; *UniVibes*; *Vintage Guitar*.

ACKNOWLEDGEMENTS

OWNERS' CREDITS

Guitars photographed came from the following individuals' collections, and we are most grateful for their help.
The owners are listed here in the alphabetical order of the code used to identify their guitars in the Key To Guitar Photographs below.

AH Adrian Hornbrook; **AM** Albert Molinaro (Guitars R Us); **AR** Alan Rogan; **BW** Bert Weedon; **CC** The Chinery Collection; **CD** Chris DiPinto; **CN** Carl Nielsen; **DB** David Brewis; **DE** Duane Eddy; **DN** David Noble; **EC** Eric Clapton; **GG** Gruhn Guitars; **GH** George Harrison; **HK** Hiroshi Kato; **JC** Jennifer Cohen; **JL** Jay Levin; **JSH** John Sheridan; **JSM** John Smith; **MW** Michael Wright; **NS** Nicky Skopelitis; **PD** Paul Day; **PM** Paul McCartney; **RI** Rickenbacker International Corp; **SA** Scot Arch; **SH** Steve Howe; **SO** Steve Ostromogilsky; **ST** Sotheby's London; **TR** Todd Rundgren; **YO** Yoko Ono.

KEY TO GUITAR PHOTOGRAPHS

The following key is designed to identify who owned which guitars when they were photographed. After the relevant page number (*in italic type*) we list: the guitar brand (and where necessary other identifier) followed by the owner's initials in bold type (see Owners' Credits above). For example, "*11/12*: Gibson **SA**" means that the Gibson shown across pages 11 and 12 was owned by Scot Arch.

  Jacket front: Fender **MW**. Gibson SG **TR**. Rickenbacker **AR**. Gibson Firebird **SA**. *Inside: 11/12*: Gibson **SA**. *12*: Höfner **BW**. *12/13*: Harmony **CD**. *14/15*: Gibson Barney Kessel **SH**. *15*: Gibson Tal Farlow **SA**. *16*: Rickenbacker **AM**. *16/17*: Gretsch **SA**. *18/19*: Epiphone **NS**. *20/21*: Gibson SG/Les Paul Custom **SA**. *20/21*: Gibson SG/Les Paul Standard **DN**. *21*: Gibson SG Special **SO**. *22/23*: Burns **PD**. *23*: Watkins **MW**. *24/25*: Wandré **CN**. *25*: Framus **MW**. *26/27*: Fender **AH**. *27*: Guild **DE**. *28/29*: National **JL**. *29*: Silvertone **MW**. *30/31*: Gibson **EC**. *31/32*: Gretsch White Falcon **JC**. *32*: Gretsch Princess **JL**. *33/34/35*: Gibson Firebird V **SA**. *34/35*: Gibson Firebird I white **SO**. *35*: Gibson Firebird I sunburst **SO**. *37*: Hagström **MW**, Guild Bert Weedon **BW**, Guild Thunderbird **MW**. *38*: Rickenbacker Astro **RI**. *38/39*: Rickenbacker 12-string **AR**, Kawai **MW**. *40/41*: Fender Marauder **GG**, Goya **MW**. *41*: Fender XII **NS**. *42/43*: all Strats **SA** except black p43 **ST**. *44/45*: Flying V **DB**. *44*: Gretsch **JSH**. *46*: Fender **MW**. *46/47*: Vox **PD**. *48/49*: Gibson **TR**. *50/51*: Rickenbacker 12-string **GH**, Rickenbacker 325 **YO**. *51*: Gretsch **GH**. *52*: Gibson **GH**. *52/53/54*: Epiphone sunburst **PM**. *53/54*: Epiphone natural **YO**. *55/56/57*: Fender **GH**. *56/57*: Gibson **GH**. *58/59*: all **MW**. *60/61*: Coral **SH**. *61*: Galanti **MW**. *62/63*: Fender **AH**. *64*: Aria **PD**. *64/65*: Teisco **MW**. *66/67*: both **MW**. *68/69*: Tokai **PD**. *69*: Kustom **MW**. *70/71*: Micro-Frets **CC**. *71*: Gibson **JSM**. *72*: Gibson **HK**. *72/73*: Fender **AH**. *74/75*: Ampeg See-Through **MW**. *75/76*: Ampeg black **JL**. *76* Dan Armstrong **MW**.

Principal guitar photography was by Miki Slingsby. A small number of additional pictures of instruments were taken by David Behl, Garth Blore, Nigel Bradley, Matthew Chattle, Kazumi Okuma, Sotheby's London, and Keith Sutter.

MEMORABILIA illustrated in this book, including advertisements, banknotes, books, brochures, catalogues, coins, comics, logos, magazines, newspapers, postcards, record sleeves, photographs, posters, sheet music and stamps (in fact anything that isn't a guitar) came from the collections of: Charles Alexander; Scot Arch; Tony Bacon; Jennifer Cohen; Paul Day; Dave Gregory; George Martin; *The Music Trades*; The National Jazz Archive (Loughton); Hiroyuki Noguchi; Nigel Osborne; Rickenbacker International Corp; Alan Rogan; Steve Soest; Maurice Summerfield; Will Taylor; Paul Trynka; Bert Weedon; Michael Wright. We are grateful for their permission to photograph the various items and reproduce them in this book; they were transformed for your visual entertainment by lensman Miki Slingsby.

EXISTING PHOTOGRAPHS We are grateful to the following for permission to reproduce existing photographs: Bizarre Guitars (Guyatone p41; Teisco p47); The British Film Institute (Psycho p13; Dr No p25; Sound Of Music p41; 2001 p63); Capitol Records (Beach Boys p81); Guitar Graphic (Mosrite p36/7); Colin Jones (Townshend p39); Jean-Pierre Leloir (Hendrix p44); LFI (Clapton p30); Parker Mead (Harrison p57; Beatles p80); Joe Meek Appreciation Society (Meek p77); Redfern's (Beach Boys p26; Caroline p31; Cropper p73; Dale p45; Hendrix jacket, p8, p43, p83; Jones p34; Kinks p28; Lennon p53; Muscle Beach p45; Richards p13; Spector p79; Sutcliffe/Harrison p51); Max Scheler/Stern/SOA (Liverpool groups p5); Phil Smee/Strange Things (Phillips p7); Toshiba EMI (Japan) (Blue Jeans p65).

RECORD COMPANIES We would like to thank the many record companies/labels past and present, and their staffs, who helped the factual and visual substance of this book. These include Apple, Atco, Atlantic, Buddah, Capitol, CBS, Chess, Columbia, Cotillion, Decca, Delmark, Dunhill, Elektra, EMI, Fontana, Internatioinal Artist, Island, King, Liberty, London, Marmalade, Mercury, MGM, Oriole, Parlophone, Philips, Piccadilly, Polydor, Prestige, Pye, Reaction, Reprise, Riverside, Stax, Tamla Motown, Vanguard, Verve, and Warner Bros. We are most grateful for their help.

ILLUSTRATIONS of significant people throughout the book were painted by Rob McCaig (Arai p64; Brown/Nolen p76; Fender p41; Garcia p49; McCarty p19; Moseley p37; Owens/Rich p60; Paul p21; Sullivan p29).

IN ADDITION to those already named we would like to thank: Charles Alexander; Mary-Lou Arnold (Alchemedia Productions); Andy Babiuk; Rowan S. Baker (Covent Garden Stamp Shop); Bexley London Borough Central Library staff; Julie Bowie; Steve Boyer; Harold Bradley; Dave Burrluck (*The Guitar Magazine*); Michael Carey (The Chinery Collection); Bill Carson; Walter Carter (Gibson); Chas Chandler; Scott Chinery; Piers Crocker; Mick Cushing (Type Technique); Charlie Daniels; Andy Davis (*The Beatles Book*); Paul Day; Bo Diddley; Kevin Dodd (Type Technique); André Duchossoir; Anita Gann (Sotheby's London); Lou Gatanas; John Gillard; Tommy Goldsmith; Dave Gregory; George Gruhn; Buddy Guy; Merle Haggard; John Hammel (MPL); Clay Harrell; Rick Harrison (Music Ground); Kelso Herston; John Huston; Leo Jackson; Brian Jacobs (Rittor); Etta James; Mikael Jansson; Ken Jones (National Jazz Archive); Jerry Kennedy; Michael F. Lee; Lenono Photo Archive; Brian T. Majeski (*The Music Trades*); John Majeski; George Martin; Steve Maycock (Sotheby's London); Karla Merrifield (Studio One); John Morrish; Charlie Murray; Jeremy Neech (Apple Corps); Hiroyuki Noguchi (*Guitar Graphic*); Sean O'Mahony (Parker Mead); Buck Owens; Elke Pape (Bear Family); Maurice Preece; Ian Purser; Don Randall; John Repsch (Joe Meek Appreciation Society); Alan Robinson (Demon Records); Alan Rogan; Rikky Rooksby; Klaus Schöller (Höfner); Jan Schuer (*Stern*); Glenn Snoddy; Steve Soest & Amy Soest (Soest Guitar Repair); Pops Staples; Sally Stockwell; Maurice Summerfield; Douglas Tinney (Ampex Corp); Larry Toomey (Alchemedia Productions); Paul Trynka (*Mojo*); Jaap van Eik (*Music Maker*); René van Haarlem (*Beatles Unlimited*); Mike Vernon; Robert Ward; John Welton (Redfern's); Tom Wheeler; Michael Wright; Chip Young.

SPECIAL THANKS to Andy Babiuk for useful insights into Fabs' gear, to Paul Day for unrivalled access to the 24-hour helpline, to Walter Carter for translating numbers into history, to Dave Gregory for letting us ransack his library on a regular basis, to Alan Rogan for getting this and mainly that well sorted, and to Sally Stockwell for making it all look as groovy as it gets.

PRODUCTS of the 1960s involved with this book: Hiroyuki Noguchi was produced in Saitama prefecture, Japan, 1963 by Kimiko and Kouichi; Sally Stockwell was produced in Windsor, England, 1962 by Pat and Mike; Paul Trynka was produced in Beverley, England, 1960 by Maureen and Kazimierz. Production data on 1950s products can be found in *Classic Guitars Of The Fifties*. Data on the rest of the team will unfortunately have to wait (possibly some time) for *Classic Guitars Of The Forties*.

"It's a temptation to look backwards, to select those events which showed the way things were going, and imagine that they appeared significant at the time. This is just not true."
GEORGE MELLY, 1965